SAVAGE
PASTIMES

●

SAVAGE PASTIMES

A CULTURAL HISTORY OF VIOLENT ENTERTAINMENT

HAROLD SCHECHTER

ST. MARTIN'S PRESS NEW YORK

www.stmartins.com

Book design by Jonathan Bennett

Painting on page 8, *A Descent into the Maelstrom of Edgar Allan Poe,* courtesy Joe Coleman.

Library of Congress Cataloging-in-Publication Data

Schechter, Harold.
    Savage pastimes : a cultural history of violent entertainment / Harold Schechter.—1st ed.
        p. cm.
    ISBN 0-312-28276-1
    EAN 978-0312-28276-9
    1. Violence in mass media—History. 2. Mass media—United States—History. I. Title.

P96.V52U67 2005
303.6—dc22

2004051244

First Edition: February 2005

10 9 8 7 6 5 4 3 2 1

For Ray Browne

People fall asleep at the opera—but they stay awake at a bullfight!

—TONY CURTIS IN *Houdini*

A little bit of violence never hurt anyone.

—GRAFFITI

SAVAGE
PASTIMES

●

ONE

•

I would not speak so much of myself if there were anyone
else I knew as well.

—HENRY DAVID THOREAU, *Walden*

Given the subject of this book—the perennial exploitation of graphic, "gratuitous" violence in pop entertainment—it may seem odd to begin with an epigraph from a literary classic whose most savage sequence is an epic battle between two ant colonies, and whose author expresses nothing but the most lofty contempt for the mindless ephemera of American culture. This apparent incongruity, however, mirrors the seemingly schizoid situation of my own life.

As a professor of nineteenth-century American literature, I've spent a good portion of my adult years thinking and talking about Thoreau and his contemporaries, and I've always prided myself (however pretentious this may sound) on taking certain Emersonian precepts to heart, including his insistence that the scholar speak directly from his own experience, in the first person. Of course, embracing Emerson's belief in the absolute primacy of the self is a handy philosophical stance for a narcissist. Still, I've always felt that all works of literary and cultural analysis—even (perhaps especially) those that adopt a pose of Olympian detachment—are fundamentally autobiographical. Why pretend otherwise?

So—back to me. When not holding forth in the classroom on the masterpieces of American Romanticism, I spend much of my time researching and writing mass-market true crime books about our nation's rich legacy of psychopathic sex-murder. To date, I've produced a half-dozen or so of these works, on subjects ranging from the Victorian "Arch Fiend," Dr. H. H. Holmes of Chicago—a real-life Blue-beard who dispatched an indeterminate number of victims in a sinis-ter edifice that came to be called the "Murder Castle"—to the Wisconsin necrophile, Ed Gein, the most culturally influential maniac of modern times, whose grotesque crimes have inspired countless works of contemporary pop horror, most notably *Psycho, The Texas Chainsaw Massacre,* and *The Silence of the Lambs.*

People who don't know me very well (and even some who do) tend to draw an analogy between my dual vocations and the creepily bifurcated lives of my subjects, as though I, too, lead a kind of Jekyll-Hyde existence: mild-mannered literature prof by day, author of lurid serial killer books by night. Besides the factual inaccuracy (I write in the mornings) this perception is vastly oversimplified. The disparity between my professional pursuits is not nearly as great as it seems.

For one thing, classic American literature is rife with terror and vi-olence. My classes generally begin with the New England Puritans. There's William Bradford of the Mayflower Pilgrims, contemplating the grisly tortures reportedly practiced by America's native inhabitants ("not being content only to kill and take away life, [they] delight to torment men in the most bloody manner that may be, flaying some alive with the shells of fishes, cutting off the members and joints of others by piecemeal and broiling on the coals, eat collops of their flesh in their sight whilst they live"). There is Mary Rowlandson, inventor of the "captivity narrative," recounting the wholesale slaughter of her family and friends during King Philip's War ("Another there was who, running along, was shot and wounded, and fell down; he begged them of his Life, promising them money, but they would not hearken to him, but knock'd him on the head, stripped him naked, and split open his Bowels"). There is Jonathan Edwards describing, in loving detail, the hideous suffering that awaits the unregenerate in Hell ("He will crush out your blood and make it fly, and it shall be sprinkled on His garments, so as to stain all His raiment. He will not only hate you, but He will have you in the utmost contempt; no place shall be thought fit for you but under His feet").

Later on, we encounter Phillip Freneau, the "Father of American Poetry," conveying his outrage over the enormities perpetrated on African slaves ("One with a gibbet wakes his negro's fears/ One to the windmill nails him by the ears/ One keeps his slave in darkened dens, unfed/ One puts the wretch in pickle ere he's dead"). And Charles Brockden Brown, the "Father of the American Novel," depicting his high-minded hero's reversion to wilderness savagery in his Gothic adventure, *Edgar Huntly* ("The stroke was quick as lightning, and the wound was mortal and deep. . . . The hatchet buried itself in his breast, and rolled with him to the bottom of the precipice").

When our national literature hits its stride, we find the supernatural chills of Washington Irving's *The Legend of Sleepy Hollow* (a comedy, to be sure, but fraught with genuine scares, as Tim Burton's recent film adaptation makes clear); the thrilling frontier violence of James Fenimore Cooper's Leatherstocking Tales; Hawthorne's dark allegories of satanic temptation and unpardonable sin.

Melville, of course—obsessed with the malign undercurrents of existence—portrays shattering moments of horror throughout his oeuvre: the hero's discovery of a wooden chest stuffed with human body parts near the end of *Typee,* for example, or the tearing away of a canvas tarp, at the climax of *Benito Cereno,* to reveal the butchered remains of the title character's best friend riveted to the ship's prow. And not even Hannibal Lecter is as sheerly, inexplicably evil as John Claggart, the diabolical master-at-arms in *Billy Budd,* whose personality, as Melville analyzes it, perfectly matches the profile of what we now call a criminal psychopath:

> Though the man's even temper and discreet bearing would seem to indicate a mind peculiarly subject to the law of reason, not the less in heart would he seem to riot in complete exemption from that law, having apparently little to do with reason further than to employ it as an ambidexter implement for effecting the irrational. That is to say: Toward the accomplishment of an aim which in wantonness of atrocity would seem to partake of the insane, he will direct

a cool judgment sagacious and sound. These men are madmen, and of the most dangerous sort.

Indeed, in all the range of great nineteenth-century American authors, the Transcendentalists are pretty much unique in steering clear of the horrific—at least in their writings. Real life is another story. As we know from one of his more tight-lipped journal entries, a year after the death of his first wife, Ellen, no less a luminary than Ralph Waldo Emerson snuck off to the cemetery one night and violated her grave ("I visited Ellen's tomb and opened the coffin"). Exactly what he did once he pried off the lid and found himself face to mouldering face with his long-dead beloved we will never know. What we can say for sure is that, at the very least, the great preacher of Ideal Beauty and Reason once engaged in an act of necrophiliac desecration worthy of one of Poe's demented protagonists.

And speaking of Poe. I sometimes wonder how it is that—in an era when everything from *Huckleberry Finn* to *Harry Potter* is banned in one school district or another, and when the public is so concerned about the kind of violent fantasies peddled to children—Poe's fiction, as far as I know, has never elicited a peep of protest from the usual moral watchdogs. Parents who get livid over gangsta rap and violent video games have no apparent problem with allowing their kids to read stories filled with the most extreme acts of sadism: men who cut out the eyeballs of their favorite pets ("The Black Cat"), or subject their rivals to the unspeakable torture of living interment ("The Cask of Amontillado"), or butcher their housemates for no compelling reason and dispose of the reeking remains beneath the floorboards ("The Tell-Tale Heart"). There's no getting around the fact that this is exceptionally gruesome stuff. Why is it even permitted in the classroom?

When I pose this question to my students, they reflexively answer, "Because it's art," without really considering the full implications of that statement. One implication is that art and intensely disturbing images of horror and violence are not incompatible—a truism verified by even a cursory glance at great literature, from *The Iliad* to *A*

Light in August, The Inferno to *Crime and Punishment, Beowulf* to *Native Son*, Chaucer's "Prioress' Tale" to any number of Shakespeare's works. (Watching Cornwall put out Gloucester's eyes in a production of *King Lear* I saw many years ago at Lincoln Center remains the single most traumatizing moment of my theater-going life; and nothing in all the *Friday the 13th* movies combined can equal the appalling horrors of *Titus Andronicus,* in which a young woman, after being brutally raped, has her hands chopped off and tongue cut out by her assailants, who are later butchered and baked into a pie which is fed to their mother.)

Incest, rape, cannibalism, torture, homicide in all its myriad forms (matri-, patri-, regi-, infanti-, etc.)—the classics are packed with this stuff. So, by the way, are many world-famous paintings, a fact that can be easily confirmed by a look at Lionello Puppi's stunning volume, *Torment in Art,* which reproduces dozens of harrowing masterworks, from Rembrandt's *The Blinding of Samson* to Goya's *Woman with her Throat Cut.*

Indeed, so pervasive are such grisly doings in the masterpieces of

Western literature that one eminent critic, Leslie Fiedler, has gone so far as to suggest that great books endure precisely *because* they allow readers to indulge vicariously in the most taboo fantasies. "Such honored works as Sophocles' *Oedipus Rex,* Euripides' *Medea,* Shakespeare's *Macbeth,*" he claims, "have persisted not merely because they instruct us morally or delight us with their formal felicities, but because they allow us, in waking reverie, to murder our fathers and marry our mothers with Oedipus; to kill a king with the Macbeths, or our own children with Medea . . . and to glory in it!"[1] Samuel Richardson—the eighteenth-century author whose books *Pamela* and *Clarissa* are considered the first modern novels—took such a dim view of the "vicious behavior" portrayed in the classical epics that he blamed poets like Homer for much of the bloodshed in the world. "Would Alexander, madman as he was, have been so *much* a madman, had it not been for Homer?" he writes in his novel *Charles Grandison.* "Of what violences, murders, depredations, have not the epic poets been the occasion?"

That great literature offers something besides Beauty and Truth—

that it also provides an escape into realms of forbidden experience—is a difficult notion for many people to accept. Certainly my students are engaged in a form of denial when they insist on invoking the talismanic word "art" to explain the potent appeal of Poe's best-known tales.

Of all the great American writers of the mid-nineteenth century, Poe is far and away the most widely read by modern audiences, and it's definitely not the "formal felicities" of his writing (to use Fiedler's phrase) that accounts for his appeal, nor the "moral instruction" offered by his fiction. His prose is often overwrought to the point of near-unintelligibility, and the only moral to be gleaned from a story like "The Fall of the House of Usher" is the inadvisability of entombing your sister alive. Hawthorne is a far more graceful stylist, and his themes are more wide-ranging and profound. And yet, even today, a literate teenager is far more likely to have read some of Poe's stories for pleasure than, say, "Young Goodman Brown" or "The Minister's Black Veil."

There's only one explanation for this state of affairs: the over-the-top, sadistic violence of his most famous tales. Some of the more squeamish admirers of Poe have found it necessary to apologize for the gruesome excesses of his imagination. "Poe must have been considerably disturbed mentally by the kind of imagery and incident which he had found forced upon himself, by the dictates of his own nature, in the *Tales of the Grotesque and Arabesque,*" writes Hervey Allen in his exhaustive biography, *Israfel.* "He could not fail to recognize that many of the implications of these stories were distinctly abnormal, particularly those which reveled in the horrible rendings of human flesh, blood, and the strange sex or sexless relations of the heroes and heroines."[2]

It seems dubious, at best, to claim that Poe must have been "considerably disturbed" by the content of his own stories. Clearly Allen is talking about his own feelings. In any case, what keeps Poe's stories alive for contemporary readers (and filmmakers, comic book artists, and other pop creators who continue to draw on his work) is precisely

the "distinctly abnormal" goings-on that high-minded scholars like Hervey Allen tend to find so distasteful.

Poe himself was fully aware of the popular appeal of the horrific. In an oft-quoted letter to one of his employers, the publisher Thomas Wilkes White, he pointed out that the most successful magazines on the market were those that printed stories like his own "Berenice" (the heart-warming tale of a young man so obsessed with the dental perfection of his young female cousin that, upon her untimely death, he digs up her corpse and extracts all her teeth). "To be appreciated you must be *read,*" Poe wrote to White, and what the public "invariably sought with avidity" were tales of lurid, exaggerated effect—"the ludicrous heightened into the grotesque; the fearful coloured into the horrible; the singular wrought into the strange."

Of course, Poe was not alone in this realization. Shakespeare and Marlowe understood that violence and horror were crowd-pleasers, as did Robert Louis Stevenson and Charles Dickens (whose *Uncommercial Traveler* includes a story about a man who makes his wives into meat pies). Even so rarefied a writer as Henry James appreciated the appeal of the sensational, framing his own most popular story—the supernatural chiller "The Turn of the Screw"—with a scene in which a group of friends are swapping spook-stories by the fireplace. When one of the party announces that he knows a tale that can top all the others for sheer "ugliness and horror and pain," his listeners can't wait to hear it. "Oh, how delicious!" cries one of the ladies, nicely summing up the titillating pleasure afforded by such nasty diversions.

Given humanity's innate endowment of aggression and cruelty— an instinctual inheritance from our archaic past—it's no surprise that we require outlets for our bloodthirsty tendencies, for what Henry James's brother, William, called "our aboriginal capacity for murderous excitement."[3] After all, as a species we've been "civilized" for only a few millennia, compared to the many millions of years we existed as savage hominids who lived by hunting and slaughter. As Carl Sagan puts it, "After 10,000 generations in which the killing of animals was our hedge against starvation, those inclinations must still be with us."[4] The psychological ramifications of this evolutionary reality were laid out by Freud in his seminal study, *Civilization and Its Discontents.* The simple—if "eagerly denied"—truth, Freud writes,

> is that men are not gentle, friendly creatures wishing for love, who simply defend themselves if they are attacked, but that a powerful measure of desire for aggression has to be reckoned as part of their instinctual endowment. The result is that their neighbour is to them not only a possible helper or sexual object, but also a temptation to them to gratify their aggressiveness on him, to exploit his capacity for work without recompense, to use him sexually without his consent, to seize his possessions, to humiliate him, to cause him pain, to torture and kill him. *Homo homini lupus* ["Man is a wolf to man"]— who has the courage to dispute it in the face of all the evidence in his own life and in history?[5]

This rapacious part of ourselves—the flip side of our civilized personas—has been called many things: the Id, the Shadow, the Other, the Alter Ego, Mr. Hyde. Many people staunchly refuse to accept its existence, at least in themselves. To them I would merely quote the following lines from Emily Dickinson, a genius who—despite the evident blandness of her outer life—had an exceptionally clear-eyed view of the dark and tragic complexities of the human soul:

> *One need not be a Chamber—to be Haunted—*
> *One need not be a House—*
> *The Brain has Corridors—surpassing*
> *Material Place—*
>
> *Ourself behind ourself concealed—*
> *Should startle most—*
> *Assassin hid in our Apartment*
> *Be Horror's least.* [6]

That one of the central functions of art—and especially popular art—is to satisfy the socially unacceptable cravings of this hidden, primitive part of ourselves is Leslie Fiedler's point: "What all truly popular writers seem to know, or perhaps better to intuit," he says, "is that any system of morality becomes finally irksome even to its most sincere advocates, since it necessarily represses, suffocates, certain undying primal impulses which, however outmoded by civilization, need somehow to be expressed. And this release of the repressed, all art which remains popular, whatever its critical status, makes possible." [7]

Others critics have put it differently, though they reach essentially the same conclusion—that popular art offers a safe, socially acceptable way to gratify the "carnivore within" (as William James called the atavistic self that persists beneath the surface of our dutiful daily lives). Stephen King, for example—whose nonfiction book, *Danse Macabre,* is one of the most astute analyses of the horror genre ever written—offers a characteristically colorful metaphor to convey this idea, comparing the psychological experience of pop horror to "lifting a trapdoor in the civilized forebrain and throwing a basket of raw meat to the hungry alligators swimming around in that subterranean river beneath."[8] (And, of course, it's not just horror that feeds our less decorous selves but all forms of pop fantasy, including romance, which, under a heavy sugar-coating of sentimentality, celebrates all kinds of taboo behavior—a hot weekend of adultery with a dashing photographer, for example, while your husband is away on a trip.)

Though taken from a different context, my own favorite metaphor for the phenomenon I'm discussing comes from D. H. Lawrence's brilliantly eccentric book, *Studies in Classic American Literature,* in which he says: "The soul of man is a dark forest."[9] We moral law-abiding folk are trained, from earliest infancy, to walk a straight and narrow path, not only in our daily lives but through the wilds of our own imaginations. There are unlovely places in our minds that we're cautioned against investigating, or even acknowledging. "Don't go there," we are warned when we threaten to express any improper thought. Needless to say, these dark, forbidden regions exert an irresistible attraction. It is the main purpose of pop entertainment to give us safe passage into these shadowy borderlands, to allow us to explore, like the heroes of fantasy and fairytales, the black forests of our own underminds, where everything uncivilized—cannibals, witches, werewolves, ogres, and all the other monstrous avatars of our own ancient lusts and aggression—resides.

Fairy tales, in fact, are very much to the point here. When I argue that people take pleasure in stories filled with sensational violence and horror, I don't, of course, mean every single person in the world, but humanity in general. And part of my evidence for this sweeping assertion is narrative folklore—the stories that have delighted human beings throughout the ages.

It is common nowadays (and a sign, in fact, of our growing refinement and even fastidiousness as a culture) to think of folk stories as quaint and charming kiddie tales with uplifting morals. In point of fact, they tend to be exceptionally crude and grisly—so much so that one early folklore specialist, the British author Sir Laurence Gomme, flatly declared that "it is not accidental but persistent savagery we meet with in the folktale"; while a later scholar, the art critic Erwin Panofsky," identified "a primordial instinct for bloodshed and cruelty" as one of the main ingredients of folk entertainment.[10]

Anyone skeptical about the gruesome content of folklore is advised to take a look at Maria Tartar's 1987 book *The Hard Facts of the Grimms' Fairy Tales,* in which she reprints, in its entirety, an early Grimm story titled "How the Children Played Butcher with Each Other":

A man once slaughtered a pig while his children were looking on. When they started playing in the afternoon, one child said to the other: "You be the little pig, and I'll be the butcher," whereupon he took an open blade and thrust it into his brother's neck. Their mother, who was upstairs in a room bathing the youngest child in a tub, heard the cries of her other child, quickly ran downstairs, and when she saw what had happened, drew the knife out of the child's neck and, in a rage, thrust it into the heart of the child who had been the butcher. She then rushed back to the house to see what her other child was doing in the tub, but in the meantime it had drowned in the bath. The woman was so horrified that she fell into a state of utter despair, refused to be consoled by the servants, and hanged herself. When her husband returned home from the fields and saw this, he was so distraught that he died shortly there- after.[11]

The level of violence in this grotesque little tale proved too much even for the Grimms, who cut it from the second edition of their pi- oneering collection. Even so, there's plenty of horror and gore to be found in *The Complete Grimms' Fairy Tales,* from cannibalism ("Hansel and Gretel," "The Juniper Tree") to ghastly beheadings ("Darling Roland" and "The Juniper Tree" again) to hideous mutilations ("The Girl With No Hands," "Cinderella") to grisly lust murders that seem like something straight out of a low-budget slasher film (see, for ex- ample, "The Robber's Bridegroom," in which a young woman watches in horror while her boyfriend and his cohorts slaughter a kidnapped girl, then lay the corpse on a table, "cut the beautiful body into pieces, and strewed salt thereon").

The Grimms, as it happened, printed a relatively tame version of "Little Red Riding Hood." In the prototypical telling, however—as Jack Zipes demonstrates—after the wolf murders the grandmother, he butchers her body and "puts some of her meat in the cupboard and a bottle of her blood on the shelf." He then tricks the heroine into an act of cannibalism. When the child shows up with her goodies, the disguised beast tells her to stick them in the cupboard and "take some of the meat which is inside and the bottle of wine on the shelf." The heroine happily complies—whereupon the household cat disgustedly exclaims: "Phooey! A slut is she who eats the flesh and drinks the blood of her granny!" The little girl ultimately escapes by convincing the wolf that she has to go outside and (not to put too fine a point on it) take a shit.

While psychoanalytic critics interpret fairy tale violence in strictly symbolic terms—as Freudian fantasy or Jungian myth—others take it

more literally. In his book *The Great Cat Massacre,* for example, the historian Robert Darnton argues that the brutality in folktales reflects the harsh and brutal conditions of premodern societies, where vicious crime was rife (according to one authority, the murder rate in medieval Europe was "probably ten and possibly twenty times higher than in the twentieth century");[12] where wars were a constant reality and the *mutilés de guerre* were a conspicuous presence in every village and town; where public executions were a form of family entertainment; where the butchering of farm animals was a daily feature of life; and where young men celebrated certain holidays by running through the streets and slaughtering every stray cat they could get their hands on, much to the amusement of onlookers (hence the title of Darnton's book).

If—as the historical evidence suggests—people have always been entertained by torture, mutilation, horror, and gore; and if daily life in the past was far more brutal than it is today, then an interesting question is raised. "The exact contrary of what is generally believed is often the truth," observes the seventeenth-century satirist, Jean de la Bruyère. The current uproar over media sensationalism rests on two premises: that popular culture is significantly more vicious and depraved than it used to be, and that we live in uniquely violent times. Everyone seems to accept these propositions as the obvious, irrefutable truth.

But what if everyone is wrong?

TWO

·

With rare exceptions, every child in America who was six
years old in 1938 has by now absorbed an absolute
minimum of eighteen thousand pictorial beatings, shootings,
stranglings, blood-puddles and torturings-to-death from comic
books alone. The effect, if not the intention, has been to raise
up an entire generation of adolescents—twenty million of
them—who have felt, thousands upon thousands of times,
all the sensations and emotions of committing murder, except
pulling the trigger. And toy guns and fireworks, advertised in
the back pages of the comics—cap-shooters, b-b rifles,
paralysis pistols, crank 'em up tommyguns, six-inch cannon
crackers, and ray-gats emitting a spark a foot-and-half-
long—have supplied that.

—G. LEGMAN, *Love and Death (1949)*

Because of their frequent brutality, folk stories have provoked their
share of outrage over the years—condemned by overprotective parents and self-proclaimed experts as unfit for the tender sensibilities of
juvenile listeners. Back in my own boyhood, during the supposedly
halcyon days of 1950s, child psychologists issued stern warning about
the emotional perils posed by undiluted doses of the Brothers Grimm,
so that my generation was raised on bowdlerized forms of the classic
fairy tales—"Little Red Riding" with a happy ending (as opposed to
the original: "With these words the wicked wolf leaped upon Little
Red Riding Hood and gobbled her up"); "Cinderella" minus the gore
(in the authentic version, the evil stepsisters manage to squeeze into

the glass slipper by slicing off parts of their feet and are eventually punished by having their eyes pecked out by pigeons).

As for the "The Juniper Tree"—often cited by scholars as the single most beautiful tale in the Grimms' collection—it was never told to us at all, undoubtedly because the violence it portrays is positively baroque. (The story begins when a wicked mother invites her stepson to peer inside a chest, then slams the lid down on his neck, decapitating him. "Then the mother took the little boy and chopped him in pieces, put him into the pan, and made him into black-pudding." When her husband—the boy's father—comes home, she serves him the flesh pudding for supper. In the end, she meets with a gruesome, if richly satisfying, death when she is crushed by a millstone.)

Still, if we boomers were deprived of the terrifying pleasures of the uncensored Grimms, we had plenty of imaginative outlets for our wild and aggressive energies. The popular culture of the 1950s—the movies and TV shows, comic books, magazines, and even trading cards—contained a remarkably high level of horror and brutality, arguably even greater than that in today's supposedly debased and morally reprehensible commercial entertainments.

I'm aware, of course, of how heretical, if not perverse, this statement sounds. The fifties, after all, are stereotypically perceived as a Golden Age of innocence compared to our own. The mere suggestion that today's mainstream pop culture might actually be *less* violent than that of the Eisenhower years—the era of "Howdy Doody," Doris Day, and "How Much is that Doggie in the Window?"—seems preposterous on the face of it.

At the time, however—that is to say, during the fifties themselves—many intellectuals viewed "mass art" as an insidious, if not actively malevolent, force, working to corrupt the moral and intellectual fiber of the young. Comic books in particular were regarded the way violent video games are today—as a danger to the health and well-being of their school-age audience, an incitement to bloodshed and vice. In his diatribe, *Love and Death,* for example, Gershon Legman depicted comic book publishers as an odious breed, peddling pornographic violence to tender minds for the sake of the almighty buck. According to Legman's calculations, "if every American child reads from ten to a dozen comics monthly—and if there is only one violent picture per page (and usually there are more)—this represents a minimum supply, to every child old enough to look at pictures, of three hundred scenes of beating, shooting, strangling, torture, and blood per

month, or ten a day, if he reads each comic book only once."[1]

Attacks like Legman's—whose tone not only approaches the hysterical but frequently achieves it—led one historian to suggest that everyone try to put the issue in a little perspective. Writing in 1957, the British scholar Margaret Dalziel very sensibly observed that "There is a particular force in the conviction that 'popular' literature nowadays is far more depraved and degrading than that of earlier times. . . . It is widely believed that such modern publications as comics, crime fiction, and love stories of the 'true confession' type are much worse than their counterparts of former days. Yet an attempt to investigate the truth of this conviction brings one up against the fact that very little indeed is known about the popular literature of the past."[2]

Clearly, little, if anything, has changed in the decades since Dalziel wrote those words. People are still convinced that the pop culture of their own day is far more "depraved and degrading" than it used to be. And since they accept this as a self-evident truth, they never bother to do what Dalziel proposes—take a long, hard, objective look at the popular art of the past.

To say that those who rail against the "moral rot" of today's mass entertainment are guilty of sentimentalizing the past—of waxing nostalgic for the mythic "good old days"—is probably true, but overly simplistic. The mere fact that Dalziel's remarks, written nearly a half century ago, are so eerily relevant now suggests that there is something in the very nature of popular culture itself that is bound to provoke outrage, particularly in the more solemnly respectable part of the population.

And indeed, the controversy raging today over video violence and rap—and that raged fifty years ago over horror comics and rock 'n' roll—has been taking place, in exactly the same terms, since mass-produced popular art first came into existence. I have little doubt that fifty years from now, parents will be raising a howl over virtual-reality shoot-'em-ups that allow their kids to actually *feel* the splatting blood from the blown-off head of a holographic zombie, and that they will pine for the idyllic days of 2004, when children enjoyed such harmlessly cartoonish pastimes as *Resident Evil* and *Grand Theft Auto*. From the vantage point of the present—when the latest state-of-the-art entertainments seem to offer unprecedented levels of stimulation and lifelike gore—yesterday's popular culture always seems innocent and quaint.

Certainly this observation applies to the way most people view the popular culture of the 1950s, a view reinforced by such family-oriented fare as the TV show *Happy Days* and—more recently—the blockbuster movie, *Toy Story 2*. The plot of that film hinges on the discovery that Woody—the Western action figure who speaks in the voice of Tom Hanks—is actually a rare collectible from the 1950s, when he starred in a popular TV kiddie program, *Woody's Roundup,* a kind of cowboy *Howdy Doody Show.* What makes this particular Woody figure so special is that he is in such pristine condition, complete with his hand-stitched vest, polyvinyl cowboy hat, and other accessories.

Like its predecessor, *Toy Story 2* is a miracle of computer animation. Every detail of texture and movement is rendered with astonishing realism, from the plastic bumps on Mr. Potato Head's body to the elastic curl of Slinky Dog's spring.

As I watched the film, however, something struck me as wildly inaccurate. As the movie repeatedly stresses, Woody is supposed to be a perfect, museum-quality specimen of a 1950s boy's plaything. *And yet his holster was empty.* Evidently, Woody never carried a gun.

Now I understand, of course, why the powers-that-be at Disney made sure that Woody was unarmed. It's the same reason that George Lucas (much to the indignation of hardcore fans) reedited the original *Star Wars* to make Han Solo less trigger-happy, and why Steven Spielberg digitally erased the pistols from the hands of the cops in the 25th-anniversary reissue of *E.T.* and inserted walkie-talkies in their place. In our post-Columbine era, there's an extraordinary sensitivity to violent imagery among the creators of mainstream children's entertainment (a situation that can lead to ridiculous extremes, such as the test shot on the DVD version of *Toy Story* that shows Woody performing a series of fancy, quick-draw moves—flipping his six-shooter in the air, etc.—all with a nonexistent gun).

In a sense, Woody's missing firearm is a metaphor of my entire argument: that today's popular culture—particularly the movie and TV entertainment marketed to kids—is no more violent than it used to be, and in many ways (however much this flies in the face of conventional wisdom) is actually *less* so. The truth is that, in the faraway days of my own fifties boyhood, the toy and television industries promoted levels of make-believe violence that would simply not be tolerated in today's social and political climate.

It's no exaggeration to say that (as was true of nearly all my male contemporaries) guns were the single most dominant feature of my childhood play life. The plastic cowboys that constituted the dramatis personae of my own little Western fantasy land were killers one and all, some righteous, others not. True, there was the occasional lariat-twirler or bronco-buster. But the red-blooded heart of our play was the thrilling action: the shootouts and showdowns, ambushes, stage-coach holdups, and, of course, Indian skirmishes. The most coveted toy cowboys were the ones arranged in deadly shooting postures (this was in the bygone days of molded plastic, before the advent of highly articulated action figures). For added fun, you could buy little plastic badguys clutching their midriffs, having just taken one in the belly from Hopalong or Wild Bill or Kit Carson.

When we weren't sprawled on the floor, playing with our pocket-size gunfighters, we were pretending to be cowboys ourselves. Every one of the polite, studious little boys I grew up with owned an arsenal of guns. Cap guns, spark guns, water guns, guns that shot ping-pong balls, or rubber-tipped darts, or even little pellets of potato (they were called "Spud Guns," as I recall). For us, an afternoon of fun consisted of blasting away at each other with our replica Colts and arguing over who had scored a fatal shot. "Bang—gotcha—you're dead!" "No way—you missed by a mile—I shot *you* first!"

Occasionally, it is true, we varied our activities with rubber swords or tomahawks or daggers. But the main objects of our affection—and obsession—were the guns, especially the Western guns. The Pecos Kid cap pistol with silver chrome finish and faux mother-of-pearl grips. The Stallion .38 revolver with eight-inch barrel and scroll work on the frame. The trickshot Remington derringer that popped from a nickel-plated belt buckle. The cartridge-loading Ruff Rider saddle rifle. The Roy Rogers lever-action carbine with Roy's signature on the plastic wood-grained stock. The double-holstered

Wagon Train set with imitation tooled-leather gunbelt. And, of course, the *ne plus ultra* of cowboy playthings, Mattel's Shootin' Shell .45 Fanner six-gun with a revolving cylinder that chambered six brass bullets which could be loaded with "Greenie Stick-M-Caps" (a major advance over the old-fashioned, red-colored, roll-style caps that, however gratifyingly loud and smoky, made our guns look annoyingly childish and phony).

In April 2000, four kindergarten students were suspended from the Wilson School in Sayreville, New Jersey, for making their hands into guns and pretending to shoot each other during recess.[3] In the 1950s, however—when little boys (and the occasional girl) spent a significant part of their playtime brandishing die-cast pistols and pumping each other full of make-believe lead—hardly anyone batted an eye. Quite the contrary. Such violent activity was not only condoned but actively encouraged by the culture at large. And the place where it was celebrated the most enthusiastically was prime-time TV.

Self-styled moral guardians who condemn today's network TV as a major promoter of media violence have apparently not bothered to check their local listings. For several years now, the prime-time lineup on the so-called Big Three (CBS, NBC, ABC) has consisted almost entirely of breezy sitcoms, news programs, medical dramas, crime series focusing on forensic investigation and procedural matters, quiz shows, and voyeuristic reality programs. Though some of these offerings can't be defended on the grounds of good taste, even the cheesiest of them have not been guilty of portraying gun violence in a positive light, let alone celebrating it as a wholesome, red-blooded, all-American activity.

The situation was dramatically different back in the days of my own boyhood. During the 1958–59 season—when I was ten—there were no fewer than seventeen Westerns on prime-time TV, all of them rife with gunplay.[4] By my count, firearms were featured in at least six of the titles (*Colt .45, The Restless Gun, The Rifleman, Yancy Derringer, Have Gun, Will Travel,* and *Gunsmoke*). These evening programs were supplemented by daytime shoot-'em-ups targeted specifically for

younger kiddies (*Wild Bill Hickock, The Lone Ranger, Hopalong Cassidy, The Cisco Kid,* and others).

To say that the prime-time Westerns of the 1950s glorified killing is putting the case mildly. If gratuitous violence can be defined as an act of representational bloodshed that exists solely to stir up the audience, to supply them with a savage thrill, then the weekly opening of the enormously popular *Gunsmoke*—in which Marshall Dillon gunned down some anonymous guy on the main street of Dodge—certainly fit the bill. The TV westerns of my youth transformed bounty hunters (*Wanted: Dead or Alive*), hired killers (*Have Gun, Will Travel*), fast-drawing drifters (*The Texan*), and historical figures of seriously questionable character like Billy the Kid (*The Tall Man*) into bona fide heroes.

Each was identified with a special weapon that was an object of almost fetishistic attention. Palladin's custom-made revolver, encased in its chess-piece-emblazoned holster. Steve McQueen's sawed-off "mare's laig." Wyatt Earp's "Buntline Special" with its extralong barrel. The Rifleman's .44 Winchester with the specially designed ring lever that allowed him to cock it with a one-handed twirl. Yancy Derringer's eponymous handgun, concealed inside his hatband. And my own personal favorite, the uniquely designed pistol wielded by the titular hero of *Johnny Ringo*—a LeMat Special with two barrels, one firing six .45 caliber rounds, the other a shotgun shell.

And then, of course, there was Old Betsy, the legendary flintlock rifle carried by the single most celebrated idol of the televised frontier, Disney's Davy Crockett.

Unless you were there at the time, it's hard to conceive of the sheer cultural magnitude of the great Davy Crockett craze of 1954–55. No kiddie phenomenon of recent years—not the Teenage Mutant Ninja Turtles, not Pokémon, not even *Star Wars*—has come close to provoking the fever pitch of obsession that gripped America's children in the days, weeks, and months following the original broadcast of Disney's three-part *Davy Crockett* series.

Almost overnight, it seemed that every boy in the country (and a fair number of girls) was sporting a coonskin cap. So extreme was the demand for Crockett-wear fashioned from genuine fur that the price of racoon skins skyrocketed from twenty-five cents a pound to nearly eight dollars. The theme song of the show, "The Ballad of Davy Crockett" ("Born on a mountaintop in Tennessee . . ."), was recorded in more than three dozen versions (including the "Davy Crocket Mambo"), sold over seven million copies, and spent six months at the top of the Hit Parade. Every product imaginable—from belts and bedspreads to pencil cases and pajamas—was imprinted with the likeness of the "King of the Wild Frontier." Altogether, during the eight-month run of the fad, an estimated $300 million in merchandise was sold to America's children—a figure that translates into more than two *billion* in present-day dollars.

Crockett aficionados have had a field day coming up with explanations for the fad, most having to do with the usual 1950s sociopolitical realities—the Cold War, the suburban exodus, etc. What these analysts willfully ignore—but what I can personally attest to—is that we little boomer-boys went wild over Davy for a much simpler reason. The series was terrifically exciting—full of thrilling action and blood-stirring violence.

It is no accident that, in the newsreels of the day (some of which can be viewed on the supplemental material included on the Disney DVD), all the school-age Crockett wannabes are not only decked out in coonskin caps but invariably toting wood or plastic replicas of Davy's rifle, Old Betsy. Indeed, this gun was the subject of its (her?) own hit song, whose lyrics began: "Bang goes Old Betsy, my only gun is Betsy. . . ."

That the parents of America smiled indulgently while their little ones trilled a rousing paean to a deadly firearm reveals a great deal, I submit, about the level of play-violence that was regarded as acceptable fifty years ago, vis-a-vis today.

So does the series itself. Revisiting the show on DVD is an eye-opening experience for a viewer today, particularly when he recalls that the series—broadcast by ABC at 7:30 Wednesday nights on the *Disneyland* show—was targeted to the elementary school crowd (I was six years old when it premiered in December 1954). Aside from the egregious political incorrectness—the gleeful slaughter of wildlife and retrograde view of Native Americans—the televised saga contained a staggering amount of graphic violence. It is impossible to conceive of any kiddie program today that would permit the kinds of images that were transmitted to America's children by the Disney studio back in 1954 and embraced by the entire country as wholesome family entertainment.

Episode One—"Davy Crockett, Indian Fighter"—deals with Andrew Jackson's war on the Creeks. Within the first ten minutes of the program, there is a skirmish between an Indian war party and a troop of Jackson's soldiers, during which several of the latter are impaled with arrows, while Davy and his sidekick, Georgie Russell, gun down a half-dozen of the "redskin varmints," as they are generally referred to.

The action centerpiece of the hour-long episode is a protracted raid on an Indian camp that begins when two of Davy's buckskinned conmrades creep up on and dispatch a pair of Creek lookouts by slitting one's throat and stabbing the other in the back. During the ensuing battle, Davy clubs an Indian to the ground, then delivers the coup de grace with his rifle butt. He then proceeds to kill a trio of Indians with several perfectly aimed shots, while his comrades mow down an indeterminate number of braves with a fusillade from their long rifles. In the meantime, the evil chief Redstick is shown braining several combatants with his tomahawk. The sequence ends when Redstick knocks out Davy with a nonlethal hatchet blow that leaves the hero's scalp visibly bleeding. When the smoke finally clears, we see the battleground littered with corpses.

In the climactic sequence of Episode One, Georgie is captured by the Indians and tied, half naked, to a stake. Just as he is about to be burned alive, Davy appears and challenges Redstick to a bout of man-to-man combat, which is conducted with tomahawks and war clubs.

Though Episode Two—"Davy Crockett Goes to Congress"—features a very satisfying knock-down-drag-out, no-holds-barred brawl between Davy and a backwoods braggart, it is relatively devoid of action, which made it the least favorite segment of the series, at least among my own friends. The relative lack of violence in Episode Two, however, was more than made up for by the concluding hour of the series, "Davy Crockett at the Alamo," whose level of carnage remains unsurpassed in the history of televised children's entertainment. Watching it again on DVD, I was stunned by the sheer brutality of the battle sequences, which featured more deaths by sword, bayonet, knife, pistol, and rifle than can possibly be counted. In one especially poignant moment, a bedridden Jim Bowie heroically meets death by plunging his blade into the back of an enemy soldier while being bayonetted in the gut by a horde of enraged Mexicans.

Shootings, stabbings, scalpings, stranglings—it was all just as Gershon Legman reported, and not just in crime comics but on network TV! And what was the psychological effect of this constant barrage of media violence on us baby boomers? Legman predicted that it would turn us all into sociopaths, into a generation of junior Dilingers and de Sades. Instead, we grew up to be the generation that preached (however sanctimoniously) peace, love, and flower power, and believed we could end the Vietnam War by surrounding the Pentagon and chant-ing "Om." The same kids who had spent their childhoods shooting each other with die-cast revolvers and plastic flintlocks grew up to be teenagers who engaged in such violent activities as lying around their crash pads and staring at lava lamps.

THREE

•

*If one of today's comic-book heroes could step into the pages
of a dime novel, he'd probably faint dead away before the
end of the first chapter. The heroes of these old-style thrillers
wallowed in pools of blood that would have frightened
Superman.*

—RAYMOND L. ANDREWS, *"Grandfather Liked
Them Gory"*

Judged by the standards of contemporary kiddie programming, the
Davy Crockett TV series was remarkably strong stuff. At the time of its
initial broadcast, however, it was criticized for the opposite reason.
Historians and other commentators complained that it was overly
tame—that it presented a misleadingly sanitized portrait of the famous
backwoodsman. And there was a legitimate basis for this charge. Compared to the legendary Crockett of a hundred years earlier, the figure
portrayed by Fess Parker in the Disney version was a frontier Goody-
two-shoes, a Boy Scout in buckskins.

Following his death at the Alamo in 1836, the real-life Crockett was
immortalized in a series of enormously popular almanacs whose pages
of practical information—weather predications, lunar charts, astro-
nomical calculations, etc.—were interspersed with colorful anecdotes
about Davy's ostensible exploits. These cheaply made pamphlets—
illustrated with woodcut engravings—were among the best-selling
publications of their time, devoured by adults and children alike. As
such, they afford a good deal of insight into the tastes and sensibilities
of the American public circa 1850. And what they reveal is that our

popular culture in the pre–Civil War era was, if anything, far more replete with brutality than it is today.

Take, for example, one of the supposedly uproarious tales that appear in the *Crockett Almanac* of 1839. Written in the comical backwoods dialect that tickled audiences in Mark Twain's era but that often seems barely intelligible now, it is titled "A Scentiferous Fight with a Nigger."

"I had just got afloat on the Great Bend, in my Alleghany skiff, and was about pushing off, when I seed the reeds bending most double, a trifle from the landing place," the story begins. "So I brought my rifle to bear and was just about getting a blizzard on the cretur, when it popped up its head, and I seed by the wool on the skull that it was a pesky great bull nigger."

Apart from Web sites maintained by white supremacist neo-Nazi hate groups, it would be hard to find racist sentiments as poisonous as the ones conveyed in this tale, which—in 1839—was chuckled over as wholesome family fun by mainstream America. Equally shocking to the modern reader—and more pertinent to my own concerns—is the unmitigated savagery that the story exults in.

When the stranger (variously referred to in the text as "Blackey," "Mr. Nig," "snow-ball," and simply "the nigger") leaps aboard Davy's skiff, the two men engage in a ferocious battle that only ends when our all-American hero gouges out his opponent's eye—a tactic he takes great pleasure in describing, down to the sensation in his thumb as he digs it deep into the man's socket:

In the first place I ketched him by the wool and jerked out two hands full, which made him feel quite unpleasant. He then run off and kum at me with his head. He got hold of my two ears and gave me a butt right in the front part of my head, that almost blinded me, for the feller's skull was as hard as the two sides of an iron pot. So I got one of my ears out of his infernal black paw, and then I got two good blows at him with my feet on his shins. That made him so mad that he run his fingers right up my nostrils. I didn't mind that much, for it shut out the enduring bad smell which the cretur had about him when he got fairly warm. So we wrassled and jerked and bit for a long time, till I got a chance at one of his eyes with my thum nail. Then when I begun to put on the rail Kentucky twist, he knew it was all day with him, and he fell on his knees and begged for mercy. His eye stood out about half an inch, and I felt the bottom of the socket with end of my thum.[1]

The illustrations that accompanied these ostensibly comic little yarns were equally graphic in their brutality. The engraving reprinted below, for example—also taken from the 1839 almanac—shows the head of a decapitated pirate (complete with exposed neckbone) impaled on a bloody stake and circled by a vulture that is hungrily eyeing the ghastly thing.

In spite—or rather precisely because—of the exceptionally crude and brutish nature of the Crockett almanacs, there is a fair amount to be learned from them. Anyone inclined to believe that the popular culture of nineteenth-century America was more refined than today's will be instantly disabused of that notion by even a glance at their pages. Indeed, anyone who insists on imagining that the country itself was a gentler, more innocent place 150 years ago will have to rethink that position, since it's safe to assume that only a cul-

ture steeped in violence and vulgarity—not to mention virulent racism—would have regarded such material as hilariously entertaining.

(Of course, there's no reason to turn to the Crockett almanacs to verify the latter point, when the same lesson can be garnered by reading *The Adventures of Huckleberry Finn*—a masterpiece revered, among other reasons, for its realistic portrayal of life in the antebellum South. In the relatively brief span of time covered in the book, the thirteen-year-old hero is exposed to an astonishing amount of barbarity: murders, gun duels, blood feuds, lynch mobs, tar-and-featherings—to say nothing of the horrors of slavery. In addition to its other virtues, the book is a useful reminder of just how sheltered our lives are today, compared to the everyday savagery that Huck is accustomed to.)

After two decades of delighting the public with richly diverting tales of manslaughter, mayhem, and bodily mutilation, the Crockett almanacs disappeared from the marketplace in 1856. Four long years would pass before the youth of America found a suitable replacement, a new brand of printed entertainment to supply its insatiable need for stories of violent adventure. This type of publication was called the dime novel, and it quickly became not only the most successful but also the most controversial pop product of its time—the direct forerunner of all the commercial kiddie entertainments that have caused such moral consternation in our own era, from 1950s horror comics to contemporary video shooter games.

The dime novel was born in the summer of 1860, when the New York publishing firm of Beadle and Adams put out a cheaply made paperbound adventure story—Ann Sophia Stephens's *Malaeska, the Indian Wife of the White Hunter*—and priced it at ten cents. ("A dollar book for a dime!" was Beadle's advertising slogan.) Within a few weeks of its appearance, Mrs. Stephens' novel had sold more than sixty-five thousand copies. Beadle immediately followed up with other crudely printed page-turners, published at the rate of two per month. When the eighth title in the series—Edward S. Ellis's *Seth Jones; or, The Captives of the Frontier*—appeared in October 1860, the American public snapped up nearly half a million copies.

Before long—as other publishers began churning out scores of these throw-away publications—the marketplace became flooded with them. During the Civil War they were shipped by the freight car load to Union soldiers, who—starved for escapism—devoured countless works like *Fugitives of the Border*, *The Phantom Horseman*, and *Bald-Eagle Bob, the Boy Buccanneer*

The product of underpaid and largely talentless hacks, these outlandish fantasies might not have offered much in the way of convincing characters, credible stories, plausible dialogue, or anything resembling literary merit. But—with their extravagant tales of heroic frontiersman, savage "redskins," swashbuckling pirates, and romantic desperadoes—they did offer the kind of easy, fast-paced thrills that, in a subsequent era, would be supplied by superhero comics, television westerns, and action movies. And like those later forms of pop entertainment, they soon came under attack by assorted moral watchdogs—politicians, religious leaders, educators, and the like.

Denunciations of the dime novel's supposedly corrupting effects on young minds began appearing everywhere, from the pulpit to newspaper editorial pages to such venerable publications as *Harper's* and the *Atlantic Monthly*. Writing in the late 1870s, for example, a critic named W. H. Bishop blamed everything from school truancy to petty thievery to parricide on the "sensational romances" peddled in "cheap dime fiction." And in a famous editorial cartoon of the time, a dime

PISTOLS

A NICE PISTOL!!! GIVEN WITH EVERY YEAR'S SUBSCRIPTION!

novel publisher is shown giving away a free loaded pistol to every young subscriber. The implication was clear: Beadle and his ilk were little more than merchants of death, turning innocent children into cold-blooded killers.

To be sure, there were other commentators who came to the defense of dime novels, most notably a critic named William Everett who—writing in the distinguished cultural journal *The North American Review*—declared that these crude, wildly popular books "were unobjectionable morally, whatever fault be found with their literary style and composition. They do not even obscurely pander to vice, or excite the passions."

Similarly, Edmund Pearson—an early historian of the genre— scoffed at the notion that dime novels were responsible for polluting the morals of the young. To Pearson, the dime novel merely served as a scapegoat, a simple explanation for the troubling complexities of human behavior (and—for young delinquents and their parents alike—a handy way of shirking blame).

"Parents who had shamefully neglected a son and allowed him to stray into mischief," he wryly observed, "found it very convenient to stand in a police court and lay all the blame on dime novels. Inherent deviltry; neglect; selfishness; cruel egotism—oh, dear, no. It was nothing but wicked dime novels. Willy was such a good boy until he began to read them. . . . Judges and teachers and clergymen and Sunday-school superintendents and even police chiefs began to denounce dime novels. It was the most useful explanation of crime, and the easiest excuse for the offender."[2]

Erasmus Beadle himself insisted on the purity of his publications, issuing a set of guidelines to his authors that prohibited "all things offensive to good taste," forbade any "subjects or characters that carry an immoral taint," and warned against stories that "cannot be read with satisfaction by every right-minded person, young and old alike." And it was certainly true that readers would have been hard-pressed to find anything even remotely suggestive in a work like *Antelope Abe, the Boy Guide* or *Mohawk Nat: A Tale of the Great Northwest.*

Violence, however—of the ostensibly wholesome, red-blooded, all-American variety—was another matter. As cultural historian Russell Nye has written, the Beadle books were crammed with "blood, bullets, and constant frantic action."[3] According to Nye's estimate, the typical dime novel averaged about twenty killings per book. And the situation became even more extreme as other publishers entered the field and began issuing ever more graphic and sensationalistic stories. To keep up with competitors like George P. Munro, the Beadles were forced to boost the bloodshed in their own publications—"to kill a few more Indians," as Erasmus Beadle put it. Before long, the level of violence in books like *Redplume the Renegade, Rangers of the Mohawk,* and *Rattlesnake Ned's Revenge* had reached a dizzying pitch.

In his attack on "cheap dime fiction," W. H. Bishop estimated that among the dozens of books he had purchased while researching his study, "there were not less than ten thousand slain." He then goes on to describe the carnage in one of the most popular dime novels of all time, Edward L. Wheeler's *Deadwood Dick on Deck; or, Calamity Jane, The Heroine of Whoop-Up:*

> In the first chapter, seventy road-agents come riding into town. They slay eighteen of the residents and are slain themselves—all but one, who is, by the orders of a leader named Old Bullwhacker, im-

mediately strung up to a tree and pays the earthly penalty for his crimes. And in the next chapter, we find a young man named Charley Davis dashing around a bend, bestriding his horse backwards, and firing at five mounted pursuers. They were twelve originally, but he has gradually picked off the rest. He is joined by Calamity Jane, a beautiful young woman who carries a sixteen-shot Winchester rifle, a brace of pistols in her belt, and another in her holsters, and between the two the pursuing five are easily disposed of. Here are a hundred dead in two chapters only!

In a similar vein, Russell Nye cites a typical passage from one of the later Beadle novels in which the hero—having stumbled upon "the swollen, mutilated corpse of a man, covered with blood and clotted gore"—notes how "the distorted countenance was rendered doubly repulsive by the red streaks where mingled blood and brains had oozed from the shattered skull."

Clearly, the media violence so often deplored by contemporary critics pales by comparison to the slaughter commonly found in dime novels—those immensely popular, escapist entertainments of the pre– and post–Civil War era, whose primary audience was young boys. As journalist Raymond Andrews put it in a 1950 *Esquire* piece on dime novels: "Sure they were gory. But Grandfather liked them that way."[4]

American boys weren't the only audience for sensationalistic schlock during the late nineteenth century. In Britain, their juvenile cousins were devouring countless of so-called "penny dreadfuls"—a term indicative of both the cut-rate cost and quality of these tacky publications and the frequently appalling content of their stories.

Like *Seth Jones, Deadwood Dick on Deck,* and other dime novels, the penny dreadfuls of the Victorian era specialized in escapist fantasies with a heavy emphasis on frenzied action and graphic gore. If anything, these lurid entertainments—which were aimed primarily at working-class youngsters, mostly (though not exclusively) boys—were even more wildly violent than their American counterparts. Besides celebrating

Kiddie Lit, 1860s Style

•

Among the more than three thousand titles published during the life span of the dime novel, the most perennially popular among young readers was the wilderness adventure, *Seth Jones: or, the Captives of the Frontier.* Its creator was Edward Sylvester Ellis, an author so insanely prolific that, by comparison, Stephen King is a sluggard and Joyce Carol Oates a victim of writer's block. In the course of his career, Ellis published 150 dime novels under his own name, plus an indeterminate number under fifteen different pseudonyms. And that was just for the publishing house of Beadle and Adams. Ellis also churned out books for many other publishers, including a nine-volume *Library of American History* illustrated with 1,200 pictures.

Of this astonishing output, *Seth Jones* remains his best-known title. An instant smash among America's juvenile readers, it is reported to have sold an astonishing 450,000 copies within the first six months of its initial publication in 1860. The story—a frontier thriller in the mold of James Fenimore Cooper's *The Last of the Mohigans*—takes place in western New York at the end of the Revolutionary War. In the following passage—which gives a fair idea of the kind of graphic gore commonly found in dime novels—the hero comes upon a victim of Indian torture whose hideous remains are described in sickening detail. Apart from its sheer gruesomeness, the passage reflects the same inveterate bigotry that infects the Crockett almanacs, as seen in Seth's reaction when he discerns the race of the victim:

It was while he stood thus, eagerly scanning the valley, that his looks were suddenly attracted toward a point near the center of the valley, from which a faint, bluish wreath of smoke was curling upward. Seth watched for a while, until he felt he could not understand the meaning of it without venturing into the valley. This conclusion arrived at, he hesitated no longer, but descended and entered at once the luxuriant undergrowth.

When fairly within it, he made a detour to the right, so as

(continued)

to pass around the fire, and to avoid the path that one unsuspicious of danger would be apt to follow. As he made his way slowly and cautiously forward he paused and listened intently. Finally he judged that he must be near the fire that had excited his apprehensions. The snapping of a burning ember guided him, and a few minutes later he stood within sight of it.

Here he met with a sight that chilled him with horror!

Some wretched human being was bound to a tree and had been burned to death. He was painted black as death, his scalped head drooped forward, so that, from where Seth stood, it was impossible to distinguish his features; but he saw enough to make him shudder. Every vestige of the flesh was burned off to the knees, and the bones, white and glistening, dangled to the crisp and blackened members above! The hands, tied behind, had passed through the fire unscathed, but every other part of the body was literally roasted! The smoke in reality was the smoke from this human body, and the stench, which was now horrible, had been noticed by Seth long before he suspected the cause.

"Heavens and earth!" he muttered to himself, "this is the first time I ever saw a person burned at the stake, and I hope to God it will be the last time. Can it be a *white man*?"

After some cautious maneuvering, he gained a point from which he could obtain a view of the face, and he experienced considerable relief when he discovered it was not a white man.[5]

the exploits of outlaws, thieves, and murderers—who were invariably cast as Robin Hood–style heroes—they often focused on the crimes of psychopathic killers, whose atrocities were recounted in hideous detail.

One of these monsters was the infamous Sawney Beane. Born during the reign of James IV of Scotland, the sociopathic Beane and his common-law wife fled from civilized society and found refuge in a cave on the Galloway coast, where they proceeded to spawn a family that—through years of incestuous breeding—eventually grew to forty-eight members. The main component of their diet was human flesh. Preying on unwary travelers, the feral clan not only robbed but cannibalized their victims, "butchering them in their den, then salting and pickling the meat for future consumption," as Michael Anglo writes in his colorful history, *Penny Dreadfuls and Other Victorian Horrors.*[6] Eventually, the Beanes were rounded up by a small army led by the Scots king himself,

"NELLY STARTED BACK IN HORROR."

who condemned them to a punishment commensurate with their crimes. "The sex organs of the men were cut off and cast into a fire, and their hands and legs severed from their bodies," Anglo explains. "They were left to bleed to death while the females were forced to watch. Finally, cursing and swearing, the women were thrown into fires and slowly burned to death."

This staggeringly gruesome story became the basis for a popular penny dreadful, *Sawney Beane, the Man Eater of Scotland,* that was published in one hundred and four serialized installments, beginning in 1825.

Another cannibalistic killer whose ghastly exploits thrilled young Victorian readers was Sweeney Todd, the legendary "Demon Barber of Fleet Street." Best known nowadays as the vengeful hero of

Stephen Sondheim's acclaimed musical, Sweeney was a wildly popular figure among working-class readers of the Victorian era—so much so that (according to one cultural historian) the very word "barber" fell into disrepute among genteel Londoners, who did not wish in any way to be associated with the vulgar masses and took to using the term "hairdresser" instead.[7]

Sweeney first entered pop culture in 1846 as the star of a serialized novel with the improbably innocuous title, *The String of Pearls: A Romance*. Written by a prolific hack named Thomas Peckett Prest, it appeared in a weekly penny-paper, *The People's Periodical and Family Library*.

In Prest's version, Sweeney is a harmless-looking fellow, who—motivated by sheer blood lust—slits the throats of his customers while shaving them in a sinister barber chair. When activated by a hidden bolt, the chair flips backwards, pitching the bodies through a trap door into the basement, where they are butchered and made into meat pies which are sold by his neighbor, Mrs. Lovett. Though her customers occasionally discover peculiar ingredients in their pies—from human hairs to thumbnails to brass buttons—the pastries are so delectable that no one complains.

"And well did they deserve their reputation, those delicious pies!' writes Prest.

> There was about them a flavour never surpassed and rarely equalled; the paste was of a most delicate construction and impregnated with the aroma of a delicious gravy that defied description. Then the small portions of meat which they contained were so tender, and the fat and the lean so artistically mixed up that to eat one of Lovett's pies was such a provocative to eat another that many persons who came to lunch stayed to dine.

Prest also took great pleasure in conjuring up the dreadful stench that emanated from the subterranean oven where Sweeney's victims were rendered into pie filling:

About this time and while these incidents of our most strange and eventful narrative were taking place, the pious frequenters of Old St. Dunstan began to perceive a strange and most abominable odour throughout the sacred edifice.

It was in vain that old women who came to hear the sermons, although they were too deaf to catch a third part of them, brought smelling bottles and other means of stifling their noses; still the dreadful charnel-house sort of smell would make itself felt most painfully and most disagreeably apparent.

The discovery of Sweeney's crimes causes understandable consternation among Mrs. Lovett's customers: "How the throng of persons recoiled—what a roar of agony and dismay there was! How frightfully sick about forty lawyers' clerks became all at once, and how they spat out the gelatinous clinging portions of the rich pies they had been devouring."

At the conclusion of the story, the police enter the vaults beneath the barbershop, where they find "the heads and bones of Todd's victims. As little as possible was said by the authorities about it. But it was supposed that some hundreds of persons must have perished in the frightful manner we have detailed."[8]

SWEENEY TODD,

THE

DEMON BARBER OF FLEET STREET.

Those who complain about the deterioration of standards in contemporary popular culture might keep in mind that, in 1846, this exceptionally gruesome tale of human butchery and cannibalism appeared in a popular periodical aimed at the whole family, children included. To get a sense of what that signifies, imagine the Hallmark Channel replacing *Touched by an Angel* with a weekly show about Jeffrey Dahmer. That such a thing is, in fact, unimaginable reinforces my overarching point: that—counterintuitive as it seems—the moral tone of our mainstream pop culture may actually be better than it was in the past.

Of course, determined critics of American culture will object that—however violent they may have been—penny dreadfuls were nowhere near as bad as today's pop entertainments, because their stories were transmitted via print, not through the hyperkinetic visuals of movies and computer games, which are presumably more stimulating to the child's imagination. I will have more to say about this subject later on in this book. For now, my answer consists of two words: Harry Potter.

As that phenomenon proves, few things, even today, can excite the fantasies of children as powerfully as books. That's why young readers are such unforgiving critics of the movies made from their favorite novels. Pictures—even those produced with the latest CGI technology—simply can't match the richness of the daydreams conjured up by words. And this must have been even truer for children of earlier eras, who never saw a movie or video game. For them, the printed page *was* a Playstation, and penny dreadfuls were state-of-the art escapism, capable of eliciting a shudder or thrill every bit as intense as the kind induced by today's high-tech entertainment.

In his history of the genre, Michael Anglo vividly imagines what the experience of reading one of these lurid periodicals must have been like for a young, working-class Victorian:

> The horror of the "penny dreadfuls" must have seemed more terrifying when they were read by the flickering light of a candle or a dingy oil lamp or by the naked light of a hissing gas jet, sending grotesque shadows dancing across the walls; when thick yellow pea-soup fog blanketed the streets and chilling damp seeped through the

cracks, together with the pervasive smells of horse dung, open sewers, and rotting garbage: when the eerie sounds of clop-clopping horses' hooves and the lonely footsteps of a passer-by came muffled into the room, or when a sudden draught set the doors creaking.[9]

In any case, there was, in fact, a visual component to the penny dreadful. No issue of *The Blue Dwarf* or *The Skeleton Horseman* was complete without a few lurid engravings that invariably portrayed the most bloodcurdling moments of the story. Even the captions were creepy: "The Dead Devoured by the Living," "Burning a Witch," and "Suicide of the Murderer to Prevent his Execution."

The illustrations of a woman named Mary Byfield—who specialized in scenes of gruesome torture—were especially prized by young readers. Two typical Byfield engravings are reprinted below and on the following page. In one, a female criminal is being broken on the wheel while a crowd of spectators watches with interest; in the other, a gang of "Morlachian robbers" is roasting some Turkish prisoners on a spit.

Edward Lloyd—a pioneering publisher of cheap Victorian fiction—

once sent a note to the wood engraver who supplied the illustrations for his weekly paper, the *Penny Sunday Times and People's Police Gazette*. "The eyes must be larger," the message instructed, "and there must be more blood—much more blood!"[10]

Needless to say, the penny dreadfuls inspired the same sort of outrage that the dime novels provoked in the United States. Critics accused them of "romanticizing outlaws"; of spreading "a moral miasma through the land in the shape of the most vulgar and brutal fiction"; of "poisoning the very foundations of society" by "corrupting and inflaming the passions" of the young.

As historian John James Wilson has put it, "It was thought at the time that 'penny dreadfuls' were the origin of all youthful crimes." They were banned from respectable households and, if found in a child's possesion, they were not only confiscated but, according to Wilson, "burned without mercy"[11]—just like the skewered, flame-broiled captives in Miss Byfield's charming illustration.

FOUR

•

I'm going to give the people what they want—sensation,
horror, shocks!

—VINCENT PRICE, *House of Wax (1953)*

People who complain that American culture is going to hell in a
handbasket often single out the public's intense fascination with grisly
crime as a symptom of our ostensible moral decay. John Walsh—who
rose to celebrity as the host of Fox's *America's Most Wanted* before grad-
uating to his own morning talk show on network TV—devoted an
entire episode of the latter program to a scathing attack on so-called
"murderabilia"—morbid collectibles ranging from serial killer comic
books to locks of Charles Manson's hair. Traded on the Internet—
generally by the sort of postadolescent male oddballs who are the spir-
itual kin of die-hard Trekkies and *Star Wars* fanatics—these artifacts
were portrayed by Walsh as the height (or depth) of the immoral, and
the people who collect them as hopeless "perverts" (a term he actually
used), hardly less evil than the killers themselves.

The problem with moral crusaders, however, is an almost willful
blindness to the fundamental realities of human behavior, accompanied by a sweeping ignorance of cultural history that prevents them
from seeing supposedly unique manifestations of modern depravity
for what they really are—i.e., simply the latest versions of perennial
phenomena. Which is merely to say that, contrary to the hysterical
claims of such alarmists, there is absolutely nothing new about the
public's prurient interest in sensational crime, nor even about the de-
sire of some people to own creepy mementos. And there is certainly

nothing new about the readiness of enterprising businessmen to exploit such morbid interests.

From crucified criminals lining the Appian Way in ancient Rome, to medieval traitors left to rot in dangling gibbets, to the gunned-down outlaws exhibited in store windows and undertaking parlors in the Old West, the dead and decomposing bodies of murderers, thieves, and rapists (and sometimes of perfectly innocent victims of lynch mobs) have always been put on public display. And the law-abiding, God-fearing types who flock to see these gruesome spectacles have often felt a need to procure a little keepsake.

Exactly how long this practice has been going on is, of course, impossible to pin down, though—extrapolating from the known anthropological evidence (such as the habit of various aboriginal peoples to collect skulls, scalps, and other anatomical relics)—my best guess is forever. What we can say for certain is that as soon as canny entrepreneurs took note of this particular predilection, they figured out ways to profit from it.

In 1827, for example, Maria Marten—a young Englishwoman from the village of Polstead—vanished after supposedly eloping with a man named William Corder. The following April—acting on pleas from her mother, who had dreamed that the girl was buried beneath the floor of a local barn—police discovered the young woman's body, just where her mother had said it would be. The case became a nationwide sensation. When Corder was executed three months later, the crowd was so eager for souvenirs that the hangman's noose was cut into pieces and sold for a guinea per inch. Corder's skin was subsequently flayed from his body, tanned like cowhide, and sold piecemeal at auction. One of the larger sections ended up being made into a tobacco pouch.[1]

Of all forms of execution, beheadings generated an especially lively demand for souvenirs, particularly when royalty was involved. When

---

"Murderabelia" Through the Ages

•

Though collectors who traffic in "murderabelia" have been condemned as pathological products of our supposedly degenerate mass culture, the fact is that—as critic Michael Hollingsworth has noted—the "grisly appetite of souvenir hunters" is a "timeless" phenomenon. In his 1963 study, *The Newgate Novel,* Hollingsworth quotes from a nineteenth-century writer who noted with scorn the public's craving for mementos of notorious crimes—everything from pieces of wood from the old Red Barn in which Maria Marten was slain to the water from a well in which the body of another murder victim was dumped:

The landlord upon whose premises a murder is committed is now-a-days a made man. The place becomes a show—the neighborhood as the scene of a fair. The barn in which Maria Marten was murdered by Corder was sold in toothpicks; the hedge through which the body of Mr. Weare was dragged was purchased by the inch. Bishops' house bids fair to go

(continued)

off in tobacco-stoppers and snuff boxes; and the well will be drained at the rate of a guinea a quart.

The writer concludes with the sardonic suggestion that—given the price that such morbid souvenirs fetch on the open market—the "owner of a paltry tenement might find it worthwhile to entice a ruffian to make it the scene of a tragedy, for the sale of the planks and timbers at a crown each."

When actual relics of a murder weren't available, the public has happily settled for others sorts of souvenirs. In 1889, a Paris court bailiff named Gouffé was murdered, stuffed into a trunk, and transported to Lyons, where the horribly decomposed corpse was eventually discovered. The case became a nationwide sensation. When the killer was guillotined on February 2, 1891, a horde of spectators turned out for the beheading. To satisfy the demand for souvenirs, peddlers strolled among the crowd, selling miniature replicas of the trunk with a little lead corpse inside.

In short—apart from the fact that today's collectors of crime souvenirs and murder mementos trade and display their ghoulish treasures on the Internet—there is nothing new about the phenomenon. As the murdered Monsieur Gouffé might have put it, *plus ça change, plus ç'est la même chose.*

King Charles I was executed in 1649, his blood was mopped up with rags, which were torn to pieces and peddled to eager bystanders. Even the sawdust that had been sprinkled on the scaffold to soak up the gore was swept up and offered for sale.

During the Reign of Terror, there was an enormous demand for guillotine-related mementos. Spectators who came to enjoy the daily beheadings could go home with a souvenir program that listed the names of the condemned and was adorned with a cover illustration of a severed head above the motto, "Go to it, Lady Guillotine, give a clean shave to all those enemies of the Country!"

Fashionable women wore guillotine earrings and entertained dinner guests with "charming miniature guillotines made of mahogany. . . . Little dolls resembling one's enemies were sometimes decapitated at dessert; out spilled a red liquid into which the ladies dipped their handkerchiefs—the doll was actually a flask and the 'blood' an amber-colored perfume or liquer." And there was something for the kiddies, too: working toy guillotines, standing two feet high, that could lop off the heads of live mice and birds.[2]

For those who couldn't make it to the Place de La Revolution, there was always the Cabinet de Cire—the wax museum run by John Christopher Curtius, where visitors could see uncannily lifelike replicas of decapitated heads created by the proprietor's apprentice, a young woman named Marie Gresholtz. It was Marie—under her married name, Madame Tussaud—who would eventually turn the public's morbid fascination with grisly crime and violence into a hugely successful enterprise.

Of all the exhibits in her renowned museum, far and away the most popular has always been the Chamber of Horrors ("La Salle Sinistre," as it is known in France), which has traditionally featured not only effigies of the world's most infamous murderers but a variety of macabre artifacts. Among the attractions listed in the official 1938 souvenir guidebook are a series of "torture dioramas"; "authentic photographs of the scene of the murder of Miss Kaye"; gruesome wax heads of Marie Antoinette and Louis XVI impaled on bayonets; a replica of "Mrs. Nicholson's skull and the knife with which she attempted to injure George III"; and a full-scale copy of a medieval iron cage, complete with suffering victim. ("It is said that persons in Holy Orders who had been condemned, but were untouchable by the executioner, were placed in one of these iron cages and suspended from the Castle walls beyond the reach of all help," the guidebook usefully explains. "There they were left to endure all the agonies of thirst and hunger, the torrid heat of noonday and the numbing chill of night, until Death mercifully released them.")

Moralists who claim that there is something uniquely depraved about our current obsession with violent crime might ask themselves why—from the moment Madame Tussaud's first opened for business in 1833—visitors have always flocked in such numbers to the Chamber of Horrors, while the uplifting displays of statesmen, ecclesiastical figures, and world-famous writers attract far smaller crowds.

The popularity of Madame Tussaud's gorier exhibits wasn't lost on American showmen. Among the countless "curiosities" at his American Museum, P. T. Barnum (who made a futile bid to buy Madame Tussaud's entire collection in 1844) always made sure to feature a healthy number of macabre attractions—waxworks sculptures of infamous killers, a "rogues gallery" of criminal photographs, torture implements and murder weapons (including the supposedly genuine club that killed Captain Cook), and more. When Albert Hicks—a notorious nineteenth-century lowlife who slaughtered the entire crew of a Virginia-bound sloop—was hanged in 1860, Barnum paid $25 and two boxes of cigars for Hicks's life mask and clothing, which he promptly put on display.[3]

Many of Barnum's less reputable competitors specialized in even grislier offerings. Lower Manhattan in the Civil War era was crammed with seedy "dime museums" that displayed everything from hideously deformed humans to embalmed fetuses to macabre relics of lurid crimes. Among the "20,000 Objects of Wonder" advertised by one of these establishments, for example, were "The Head and Right Arm of Anton Probst, Murderer of the Deering Family, Amputated After Execution." To find equivalently ghoulish exhibits today, you'd have to plumb the lower depths of the Internet and check out arcane Web sites with names like Rotten.com and CelebrityMorgue.

Of course, Madame Tussaud, P. T. Barnum, and the many nameless operators of sleazy dime museums always made sure to tout their most morbid displays as highly educational experiences—a venerable ploy that allowed the public to indulge its prurient curiosity without guilt (in much the same way that paintings of nude female bodies were made safe for Victorian voyeurs by being cast as scenes from classical mythology; or that pictures of bare-breasted women could be legitimately ogled by our grandfathers in the high-minded pages of *National Geographic*).

This same hypocrisy is very much at work today on cable television, where stations like Court TV and the History Channel offer programs rife with gruesome violence under the guise of public edification. I myself once appeared in a History Channel documentary on the highly edifying topic of cannibalism, a program that—unsurprisingly, given the sensational subject matter—proved to be one of the station's most highly rated and frequently rebroadcast programs. I was also amused by an ad for the History Channel that ran in the September 23, 2002, issue of *Newsweek.* Along with a list of the week's prime-time specials (which in-

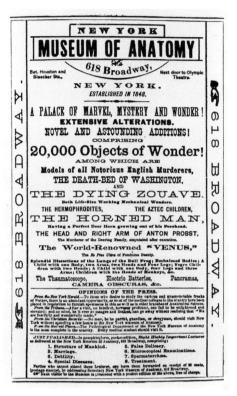

cluded a show on the death of Jesse James) the ad contained a "Weekly Quiz" that consisted of this single, historically vital question: "How many women did Jack the Ripper officially murder?"

Television, of course—along with other branches of the media—is often blamed for fostering, if not creating, a morbid interest in violence and crime. But that accusation is demonstrably false, since the public's craving for grim entertainment existed long before there was such a thing as "the media."

At least as far back as the early Renaissance, for example, tragic tales of murder, lust, and betrayal were made into songs and transmitted orally for the benefit of illiterate peasants. Many of these ballads were later transcribed by folklore scholars. Of the eight examples reprinted in the standard college textbook, *The Norton Anthology of Poetry,* one describes a father brutally slain by his daughter's new husband, who is fatally wounded in the struggle ("The Douglas Tragedy"); one deals with a young man poisoned by his lover ("Lord Randal"); one involves a woman who is hanged for the murder of her illegitimate child ("Mary Hamilton"); one relates the conversation among a trio of carrion birds as they contemplate the bloody remains of a slain knight ("The Three Ravens"); two deal with deaths by drowning ("Sir Patrick Spens" and "The Bitter Withy"); and one concerns necrophilia ("The Unquiet Grave").

By Shakespeare's time, traveling peddlers had figured out a way to profit from the public's love of sensationalism by selling printed versions of popular ballads. Some of these were the Elizabethan equivalent of supermarket tabloids, providing news of strange and shocking events, many of highly dubious authenticity. "A Marvelous Occurrence, Being the True Relation of the Raining of Wheat in Yorkshire" and "The True Report of a Monstrous Pig which was Farrowed at Hamstead" are typical titles from the late sixteenth century. Freakish births, supernatural visitations, weird and wondrous phenomena of every description were the common subjects of these crude publications.

Far and away the most popular topics, however, were gruesome crimes. Whenever a particularly ghastly murder or hideous rape occurred, it was immediately translated by some anonymous rhymester into a page-long piece of doggerel, printed on a large sheet of paper known as a broadside, and sold to the hardworking masses eager to brighten their overburdened lives with a little morbid titillation.

One such surviving broadside ballad from 1648 tells of the "Marvelous Murther Committed Upon George Drawnefield of Brampton in Derbyshire." Adorned with a woodcut picture showing the victim being slain in his bed, the ballad details the savage actions of the killers, who "broke his neck in sunder," crushed his head with "deadly blowes," then "stopt his nose and eares, his mouth and throat" with balls of dough to keep his blood from splattering all over the room. An eighteenth-century ballad called "The Cruel Gamekeeper" graphi-

cally describes the butchery of a pregnant young woman, whose fetus is cut from her womb by her barbarous lover:

> In Buxton Town in Staffordshire,
> A farmer's daughter lived there;
> On a gamekeeper, as we find,
> This damsel she did fix her mind.
>
> It happened lately in the park,
> She met her lover with an aching heart;
> She said, "My dear, what shall I do
> For I am big with child by you?"
>
> "I will not marry yet," said he,
> "For while I'm single, I am free."
> From his pocket a knife he drew
> And pierced her tender body through.
>
> He ripped her up and there was by,
> A baby in her womb did cry;

> *He then did hide among some thorns,*
> *The baby crawling in her arms.*
>
> *They took the keeper before it was long*
> *And bound him in a prison strong,*
> *And he was soon condemned to die,*
> *All on the gallows tree so high.*

The tradition of the printed murder ballad continued well into the nineteenth century, when broadsides were produced by more established printers, most located in London. The most successful was James Catnach. When William Corder was hanged for slaying Maria Marten and burying her corpse beneath the floor of the old Red Barn, Catnach ran his presses overtime, producing more than a million copies of a murder ballad that were snapped up by the public for a penny apiece. A typical verse ran as follows:

> *With heart so light, she thought no harm,*
> *   to meet him she did go*
> *He murdered her all in the barn,*
> *   and laid her body low:*
> *After the horrible deed was done,*
> *   she lay weltering in her gore,*
> *Her bleeding mangled body he buried*
> *   beneath the Red-barn floor.*[4]

Another popular ballad of the time described a ghastly case of child murder—a favorite theme of Victorian street literature. The perpetrator was a woman named Emma Pitt. Typically, the anonymous author spares the reader no detail of the grisly killing:

> *This Emma Pitt was a schoolmistress,*
> *   Her child she killed we see,*

> *Oh mothers, did you ever hear,*
> *Of such barbarity.*

> *With a large flint stone she beat its head*
> *When such cruelty she'd done,*
> *From the tender roof of the infant's mouth*
> *She cut away its tongue.*[5]

Throat slittings, stranglings, bludgeonings, and axe murder were among the many grisly subjects of these crudely written verses that were given such catchy titles as "Horrible Double Murder at Berkhamstead," "Horrible and Atrocious Murder of a Woman at Wednesbury," "Frightful Murder of the Rev. Mr. Huelin and His Housekeeper at Chelsea," "Shocking Murder of a Wife at Oving, Near Aylesbury," and "Horrid Murder Committed by Mary Wilson Upon the Body of George Benson, Through Disappointment in Marriage."

A Victorian Andrea Yates

•

Murder ballads were generally prefaced with a prose narrative providing particulars of the crime. A surviving broadside from the Victorian era, "The Esher Tragedy. Six children murdered by their mother" recounts an atrocity chillingly reminiscent of the Andrea Yates case that shocked America in June 2001:

On Friday last I was bad all day; I wanted to see Mr. Izod and waited all day. I wanted him to give me some medicine. In the evening I walked about, and afterwards put the children to bed, and wanted to go to sleep in a chair. About nine o'clock, Georgy (meaning Georgianna) kept calling me to bed. I came up to bed, and they kept calling me to bring them some barley water, and they kept calling me till nearly 12 o'clock. I had one candle lit on the chair. I went and got another, but could not see, there was something like a

(continued)

---

cloud, and I thought I would go down and get a knife and cut my throat, but could not see. I groped about in master's room for a razor. I went up to Georgy and, and cut her throat first; I did not look at her. I then came to Carry, and cut her. Then to Harry—he said, "don't mother." I said, "I must" and did cut him. Then I went to Bill. He was fast asleep. I turned him over. He never woke, and I served him the same. I nearly tumbled into this room. The two children here, Harriet and George, were awake. They made no resistance at all. I then lay down myself.[6]

Like the Yates case—and that of Susan Smith some years earlier—this horrendous act of multiple infanticide riveted the public.

As one Victorian balladmonger put it, "There's nothing beats a stunning good murder after all."

Murder ballads were popular in America, too. In the 1930s, a folklorist named Olive Wooley Burt became fascinated with this humble genre and spent the next twenty-odd years collecting hundreds of specimens, which were ultimately published in her volume, *American Murder Ballads and Their Stories*. These "tragic ditties" (as Burt called them) commemorate an enormous variety of shocking crimes, from notorious nineteenth-century serial murders (like those of the infamous poisoner Lydia Sherman, who killed her husband and all six of her children) to obscure though equally disturbing cases, like that of Naomi (nicknamed "Omie") Wise, who was gruesomely slain by her sweetheart during a riverside rendezvous:

> *He kicked her and stomped her,*
> *He threw her in the deep;*
> *Then jumped on his pony*
> *And galloped away.*
> *The screams of poor Omie*
> *Followed after him nigh,*
> *Saying, "I'm a poor sinner,*
> *Not fitten to die!"*[7]

That murder ballads continued to exert a hold on the popular imagination well into our own century was shown in a peculiar coincidence that occurred when Burt's book was finally published in 1958. In a strange twist, it appeared at precisely the time that the number-one song on the Hit Parade was the Kingston Trio's "Tom Dooley," a slick, commercialized version of a nineteenth-century murder ballad that told of a condemned young man who met his girlfriend "on the mountain" and "stabbed her with my knife."

The violence in "Tom Dooley"—though entirely gratuitous—is tame by comparison to the atrocities recounted in ballads of earlier eras. One of the most disturbing American murder ballads on record is a broadside from Oneida, New York, titled "A MOST TRAGICAL ACCOUNT of a Woman's Murder of a Peddler & Then Burning to death her Own Child." This extraordinarily gruesome poem recounts the ostensibly true case of a farm woman and her husband who invite a roving peddler to stay for the night, then slit his throat while he sleeps and steal his belongings. The next morning, their daughter goes off to school carrying a "beauteous Handkerchief" which the mother has found in the peddler's pack. The teacher so admires the handkerchief that she asks where it came from. Innocently, the child replies that "her Mother had a store/ Of articles like these." Wishing for one of her own, the teacher sends a note to the mother.

Furious at her daughter for telling the teacher about the peddler's goods—and fearful that their crime will be discovered as a result—the mother persuades her husband that they must not only get rid of the child but do so in an especially hideous way:

> They did devise the barb'rous plan,
>   That he should dig her grave;
> And she would send her to him then
>   To bury her alive!
> So when he had the grave prepared
>   The child was sent with speed;

But then he thought he could not bare
　　To do the cruel deed.

At this the Mother's anger flew—
　　She would Revenged be;
She said she'd try what she could do,
　　O what a wretch was she!

She het the oven blazing hot,
　　And then in angry Fraim
Her infants cries she heeded not,
　　But plung'd it in the flame!

The crime is ultimately detected when a visiting neighbor—noticing the stench suffusing the farmhouse—looks into the oven and finds the child's remains.[8]

Ballads weren't the only kind of crime literature available in the old days. Far from it. Both in Europe and America there was a slew of cheap publications that catered to the popular taste for lurid true crime.

In England, true crime books can be traced as far back as the 1600s. One of the most widely read works of that era was John Reynolds's *The Triumphe of God's Revenge Against the Crying and Execrable Sinn of Murther*, whose real-life tales of cold-blooded murder and equally ruthless punishment were offered under the pious pretext of demonstrating that Crime Does Not Pay—a tactic that purveyors of pop sensationalism have continued to exploit right up to the present day.

Even more popular was the Newgate Calendar—or, to use its full title, *The Newgate Calendar, or Malefactors' Bloody Register containing General and Circumstantial Narratives of the lives and transactions, various exploits and Dying Speeches of the Most Notorious Criminals of both sexes who suffered Death Punishment in Gt. Britain and Ireland for High Treason, Petty Treason, Murder, Piracy, Felony, Thieving, Highway Robberies, Forgery, Rape, Bigamy, Burglaries, Riots and various other horrid crimes and misde-*

meanors. Issued in a steady stream of new and updated editions from the late 1700s through the midnineteenth century, this collection of sordid true crime accounts was one of the most widely read works of its era—"the book, along with the Bible, Foxe's *Book of Martyrs,* and Bunyan's *Pilgrim's Progress,* most likely to be found in any English home between 1750 and 1850," as one scholar has noted.

Each entry in the New-gate Calendar recounted the crimes, inevitable arrest, and justified execution of a par-

BARBAROUS MURDER OF A CHILD BY A SCHOOLMISTRESS.

A child murder has been committed at Park Horner, in the parish of Hampreston, under circumstances of the most shocking barbarity. At the Coroner's inquest it was given in evidence that the child had been beaten on the head with a heavy flint stone, and its tongue cut completely out at the root. It was found wrapped up in another part of a drawer where the body was discovered. The inquiry lasted four hours and a-half, and resulted, in the first instance, in a verdict, "That the child was born alive and murdered by someone." The Coroner pointed out that the evidence was conclusive against Emma Pitt, the national schoolmistress, who was the mother of the child; and he expressed his surprise that such a verdict should have been returned. The Jury after reconsidering their previous finding, returned a verdict of "Wilful murder against Emma Pitt."

We have read of sad and dreadful deeds
Of mothers cruel and unkind,
But in the annals of history
Such as this we seldom find;
In the parish of Hampreston,
This deed was done we hear,
Near to the town of Wimborne,
In the county of Dorsetshire.

This Emma Pitt was a schoolmistress,
Her child she killed we see,
Oh mothers, did you ever hear,
Of such barbarity.

With a large flint stone she beat its head
When such cruelty she'd done,
From the tender roof of the infant's mouth
She cut away it's tongue!
Sad and wicked, cruel wretch,
Hard was her flinty heart,
The infant's tongue from the body was
Wrapped in another part.

The murderess placed in a drawer,
And it there, alas! was found,
The news of this dreadful murder,
Soon spread for miles around;
And first upon the inquest,
She expected to get free,

Although she was the author
Of this dreadful tragedy.
A schoolmistress too, how sad to tell,
Well known for miles around,
Who had many children under care,
In and near to Wimborne town.
Oh, what a sad example,
To children she did set,
There was never such a cruel wretch,
As the barbarous Emma Pitt.

She committed is for murder,
Soon her trial will take place,
And if she is found guilty,
How sad will be her case.
If she has a woman's feelings,
She surely will go wild.
She in such a barbarous manner killed
Her tender infant child.

The hour is approaching,
The moments near at hand,
When before a Judge and Jury,
This monster soon must stand;
And if she is found guilty,
She her deserts will get,
And mother's, miles round Wimborne,
Will remember Emma Pitt.

2 x 2   H. Disley, Printer, 57, High Street, St. Giles.   219

ticular perpetrator, whose case was summed up in a highly descriptive title: "Tom Austin. Highwayman, guilty of unparalleled butchery. He murdered his aunt, wife, and seven children. Executed in August, 1694." Or "John Stanley. An insolent puppy who presumed on his swordsmanship. Executed at Tyburn, 23rd of December, 1723, for murdering his mistress." Or "John Price, Commonly Called Jack Ketch. A rogue and liar, who was not believed when he spoke the truth. He held the office of common hangman, and was himself hanged in Bunhill Fields in May, 1718, for murdering a woman."

Like sensationalistic crime literature before and since, these shocking tales were overlaid with a thick coating of preachiness, the universal moral being the rewards of good behavior and the punishment that awaits the transgressor. The frontispiece illustration for one eighteenth-century edition shows an anxious mother handing her little boy a copy of *The Newgate Calendar,* while pointing through the window at

FRONTISPIECE.
A Mother presenting The Malefactors Register *to her Son, and tenderly intreating him to regard the Instructions therein recorded.*

Justice Wisdom Fortitude

*The anxious Mother with a parents Care,
Presents our Labours, to her future Heir;
The Wise, the Brave, the Temperate and the Just,
Who love their Neighbour, and in God who trust:
Safe through the Dangerous paths of Life may Steer,
Nor dread those Evils we exhibit Here.*

a body dangling from a nearby gibbet—an image meant to convey the message that, by taking to heart the lessons in the book, the youth might avoid a similarly gruesome fate.

The Newgate Calendar was tremendously popular not only among ordinary readers but among writers as well, influencing the work of Henry Fielding, William Thackery, and Charles Dickens, among others. It was also a source of inspiration for the artist William Hogarth, whose widely reproduced, narrative engravings—especially *The Four Stages of Cruelty*—relied on the same sure-fire formula exploited by *The Newgate Calendar:* violence and depravity masquerading as moral instruction. Presented as an object lesson in the dire end that awaits the wicked, the four-part series charts the progress of a miscreant named Tom Nero from his sadistic youth to his sociopathic manhood to his final disposition as a desecrated corpse.

Even for a modernday viewer accustomed to the explicit gore of movies like *Seven* and *Hannibal,* the sheer ghastliness of Hogarth's imagery—the hideous acts of animal torture in the first and second prints, the gaping wound of the throat-slit woman in the third, and the sickening procedure taking place in the last (in which the body of the executed killer is being publicly dissected by a team of surgeons, who are gouging out the eyes, slitting open the belly, and pulling out the guts)—is hard to stomach. The British public, however, ate it up, making him one of the most celebrated and successful artists of his time.

Nineteenth-century British artists weren't the only ones fascinated by accounts of true crime. So were some of the greatest American writers of the period, including (unsurprisingly) Poe, Melville, and especially Nathaniel Hawthorne, all of whom were avid readers of the sensationalistic publications of their day. Hawthorne was such a voracious consumer of cheap crime literature that his own son, Julian, described his father's interest as a kind of addiction—a "pathetic craving." However pathetic it may have been, it certainly reflected the tastes of his countrymen, who possessed an unappeasable appetite for true-life stories of horrible murders and ghastly accidents—a taste that the popular press was only too happy to feed.

Those who deplore the current state of American society and accuse the media of pandering to, if not actually creating, an unwholesome obsession with violence would do well to learn something about cultural history. A look at the cheap newspapers and crime literature so popular during the pre–Civil War era demonstrates quite clearly that things were no better in the past. Not only was violent crime rampant in the good old days, but the prurient need to hear every juicy detail was just as widespread and intense as it is now.

As early as 1809, for example, a New York publisher named Donald Fraser, began catering to the public's craving for horror and perversity in his monthly, *The American Magazine of Wonders,* which specialized in such ghoulish subjects as premature burial and cannibalism. Typical of Fraser's offerings, according to the literary historian David Reynolds, was the "story of a frontier family whose main food for twenty-five years is their murdered victims, or that of ferocious religious fanatics who entered a gentleman's house, bound him to a stake, violated, in his sight, the chastity of his wife and daughters; put him afterwards upon a spit, and having roasted him, compelled his lady and his children to eat his flesh and terminated the horrid scene by a general massacre of the whole family."[9]

During succeeding decades, the number of sensationalistic papers published in this country grew at a dizzying rate. By the 1850s, Emerson was complaining that his countrymen spent their time "reading all day murders & railroad accidents" in the penny papers. The taste for grisly news wasn't limited to the hoi polloi, either. Hawthorne was so enamored of the penny papers that he had a friend ship whole stacks of them to him during the years he lived abroad as United States Consul at Liverpool. And Emily Dickinson openly delighted in newspaper sensationalism, cheerfully confessing to a friend that she loved to read stories of "those funny accidents, where railroads meet each other, and gentlemen in factories get their heads cut off quite informally."[10]

Even more than horrible accidents, however, it was hideous crimes that really sold papers. No one was more aware of this fact than James Gordon Bennett, publisher of the most famous penny paper of the day, the *New York Herald.* As Bennett declared, American readers "were more ready to seek six columns of the details of a brutal murder . . . than the same amount of words poured forth by the genius of the noblest author of our times." And Bennett was ready to give the public what it wanted, providing extensive and extremely graphic coverage of the most shocking crimes of the day, like the notorious axe murder of the New York City prostitute Helen Jewett in 1836.

So extreme was the public's hunger for sensational crime stories that newspapers alone couldn't meet the demand. By the 1840s, David Reynolds notes, "almost every sensational trial, besides being played up in the penny papers, produced its own cheap pamphlet hawked in street bookstalls and railway depots." At first these crudely printed publications adopted the traditional pose of piety, presenting themselves as morally edifying works, complete with "long warnings about God's anger against criminals and man's need to beg forgiveness in the face of divine wrath." Eventually, however, they dropped all sermonizing pretense and began dishing out unabashed sensationalism in terms that bordered on the pornographic.

Anyone who doubts that nineteenth-century popular culture was at least as graphically violent as today's should consult Karen Halttunen's 1998 book *Murder Most Foul*, an eye-opening study of nineteenth-century American crime literature. As her book amply demonstrates, the cheap crime pamphlets so beloved by American readers in the 1800s are packed with the goriest details imaginable.

"Murder literature after 1800 focused overwhelmingly on images of the body in pain and death," Halttunen writes.

> The injuries of the murder victims were described in detail: "The throat was cut from ear to ear, severing the jugular veins, carotid arteries, windpipe, muscles and nerves, leaving the neckbone entirely bare." Lavinia Bacon's daughter returned from church one Sunday in 1843 to find her mother "a mangled corpse on the floor of the parlor. Her skull was literally broken to pieces—one of her eyes knocked completely out of sight and her face mutilated beyond the possibility of recognition." . . .
>
> In many murders, body-horror took the form of specific details about the state and fate of the victim's corpse. . . . The most horrifying cases of corpse disposal involved corpse dismemberment,

which had the effect of graphically prolonging the violence of the murder beyond death. *The Confession of Adam Horn* (1834) detailed how he had killed his wife with two blows of a stick, then chopped off her head and burned it, scattered her teeth in the woods, severed her limbs and buried them under an old bake oven, buried her trunk in the peach orchard, then, under fear of discovery, moved her limbs from bake oven to orchard to the attic of the house.[11]

To further milk the public's craving for gory stories, publishers repackaged these slender crime pamphlets and issued them as book-length anthologies with titles like *Record of Crimes in the United States* (1833) and *Annals of Murder, or Daring Outrages, Trials, Confessions, &c.* (1845).

As early as 1833, one enterprising American journalist, a fellow

HORRIBLE MURDER

OR

MRS. ELLEN LYNCH,
AND HER SISTER,

MRS. HANNAH SHAW,
In Federal St. near Seventh, Philadelphia,
WITH THE

TRIAL AND CONVICTION
OF

ARTHUR SPRING.

Illustrated by Engravings, by HINCKLEY, from Drawings taken on the spot.

Price, 12½ Cents.

A. WINCH, 116 Chestnut St. Wholesale Agent, Philadelphia.

named George Wilkes, had figured out an ingenious way to cash in on his countrymen's taste for violent diversion: i.e., by publishing a newspaper that eliminated all extraneous subjects—like world affairs and national politics—and concentrated primarily on sensational crime. The result was *The National Police Gazette,* a forerunner of the unabashedly lurid tabloids that would proliferate in the twentieth century. Though the *National Police Gazette* eventually evolved into a "sporting paper" with a heavy emphasis on gossip, celebrity scandal, and athletics (especially boxing), it never stopped dish-

ing up horror and gore. Each issue was lavishly illustrated with
dramatic engravings far more
slick and sophisticated than the
crude woodcuts that adorned
earlier crime publications.

The stories published in the
National Police Gazette throughout the late 1800s provide yet
another sobering confirmation
that ghastly murder—and the
public's obsessive interest in it—
has been a perennial feature of
American life. A single issue from
May 28, 1892, contains the following headlines: SHOT HER
THROUGH THE HEAD, ASSAULTED

COOKED ON A RED-HOT STOVE.
FRANK CODY, A NEW MEXICO RANCHMAN, SHOT ALMOST TO
DEATH AND THEN ROASTED ALIVE BY INDIANS.

EXECUTED BY ELECTRICITY.
LINEMAN JOHN FEEKS KILLED WHILE REPAIRING TELEGRAPH WIRES AT CENTRE AND CHAMBERS STREETS, NEW YORK.

HIM WITH A RAZOR, KILLED BY HER LOVER, and THE MURDER OF MARY WERTHEIMER'S BABY.

"Even more relentlessly grisly than the *National Police Gazette* was its British counterpart, the *Illustrated Police News,* a weekly tabloid with the largest circulation of any periodical of its time. This wildly sensationalistic paper specialized in graphically illustrated stories of atrocious murders, bizarre accidents, and the more ingenious and colorful forms of suicide (self-crucifixions were espe-

"Outraged and Crucified"

•

Typical of the lurid contents of *The National Police Gazette* was an 1894 story headlined OUTRAGED AND CRUCIFIED, about a beautiful seventeen-year-old girl named Carrie Jordan of Elliot County, Kentucky, who was gang-raped and subjected to an unspeakable torture by three male acquaintances.

"She is dead now," the article began, "and her death was a most horrific one and, what was worse, she died dishonored and shamed. She died literally crucified to the wall of a log cabin, without one friend near to help her and without one human voice to console her." The article then proceeded to give the awful details of the "fiendish crime":

The girl was but seventeen years old, and but a few days before she met her death, she started across the hills to spend

(continued)

the day with some neighbors who live two miles distant. It was a small task for this hardy girl to cover that short distance, reared as she had been in the hill-climbing country.

When she had walked half the distance, she was met by three young men whom she knew. They greeted her, and then suddenly seized and hurried her off to the depths of the forest, binding a handkerchief about her mouth to smother her screams. Despite her desperate struggles she was helpless in the hands of the young ruffians who carried her off to an abandoned log hut and ravished her repeatedly.

After ravishing her, the girl was choked into insensibility and left, presumably for dead, nailed to the wall of the building, with her arms extended in the manner of crucifixion and the nails penetrating the palms of her hands. In this position the girl was discovered, after her long absence had occasioned some alarm and consequent search, a dog trailing the way to the deserted cabin. It was several hours, and long after she had been taken home, that the girl recovered consciousness sufficiently to tell in a broken way the dreadful story of her terrible experience.

The poor victim was able to identify her assailants before succumbing to her injuries, which—"besides the ragged wounds in her hands"—included numerous blows to her body and several deep gashes in her head. A posse consisting of more than fifty men immediately set out to hunt down the three youths, vowing not to "rest till the perpetrators of the outrage are swinging between heaven and earth."

As the article confidently predicted: "There will be a lynching soon."

cially popular), served up in the usual tone of tongue-clucking piety.

To be sure, many of these articles were nothing more than the journalistic equivalent of public executions—which were, in fact, another staple of the *Illustrated Police News*. The paper was full of features with catchy titles like "Singular Method of Execution," "Lynching Four Men," and (my personal favorite) "Capital Punishments of All Na-

A MAN CRUCIFYING HIMSELF

tions," a highly educational article illustrating ways people have been tortured and put to death throughout history. ("Beheading was a military punishment among the Romans. The head of the culprit was laid on a block placed in a pit dug for the purpose beyond the *Vallum*, and preparatory to the stroke he was tied to a stake and whipped with cords.")

The frontispiece of Leonard DeVries's book, *'Orrible Murder,* a collection of pieces from this Victorian crime-and-scandal sheet, is a full-page illustration of a particularly juicy hanging in which the force of the fall has ripped off the prisoner's head. His body, meanwhile, continues to drop through the air with its hands clasped in a prayerlike gesture of last-minute repentance and a geyser of blood spurting out of its neck (a perfect visual metaphor for the paper's shameless mix of sanctimony and gore).[12]

The brutal mistreatment of women and children (the flip side of the official Victorian myth of domestic beatitude) also received regular, not to say obsessive, attention in the pages of the *Illustrated Police News*. Though the paper did take note of the occasional atrocity committed by women against men (a wife who set her husband on fire

by hurling a lamp at him during a domestic quarrel, a girl who doused her sleeping stepfather with boiling water "and when he awoke attacked him with a red hot bar of iron"), such stories were far outnumbered by accounts of "shocking cruelty" to children (beatings, stabbings, stompings, and worse) and—even more common—savage attacks on women. Every week, readers could thrill to such stories as "Frightful Wife Murder in Bristol," "Young Woman Decapitated," "Fearful Scene—Woman Torn to Pieces," "Throwing a Wife Out of the Window," "Murderous Attack on a Woman in Whitney," "Extraordinary Wife Murder," and "Murder and Mutilation of a Woman."

The engravings that accompanied these stories were seriously unsettling—more so, in many ways, than the images transmitted by even the schlockiest of today's tabloid newspapers or TV shows. The artists who provided the pictures for the *Illustrated Police News* were clearly encouraged to render each atrocity in the most graphic detail possible: husbands butchering their wives, mothers slitting the throats of their children, women cannibalizing infants, daughters scalding their fathers.

To view anything as gruesome today, you'd have to find a video store that stocked movies with titles like *Bloodthirsty Butchers, Meatcleaver Massacre,* and *I Spit on Your Grave.* A century ago, however, such wildly sadistic stuff was the mainstay of London's biggest-selling newspaper, which achieved its mass circulation by offering a surefire, time-tested commodity: morbid titillation for the common man.

FIVE

•

ANTONIO: Murder and torture; no prayers, no entreats.
PANDULPHO: We'll spoil your oratory. Out with his tongue!
ANTONIO: I haven't, Pandulpho; the veins panting bleed,
Trickling fresh gore about my fist. Bind fast! So, so.
GHOST OF ANDRUGIO: Blest be thy hand. I taste the joys
of heaven, Viewing my son triumph in his black blood.

—JOHN MARSTON, *Antonio's Revenge*

If certain entrepreneurs—like the publisher of the *Illustrated Police News*—have found ways to make money by exploiting the public's taste for sensational violence, others have taken the opposite, more high-minded tack: i.e., by offering products that present themselves as wholesome alternatives to the "pernicious trash" peddled by their competitors. Touting the virtues of his 1894 children's book, *Stories of Pioneer Days, or The Advance Guard of Civilization in America,* a writer named J. R. Jenkins proclaimed in a preface that the thrilling historical episodes found in his work were infinitely more suitable for children than the "perverting literature which is called the 'dime novel,' but is 'novel' only in being a new method of destroying the purity of the young." (At the same time, of course, Jenkins—in the time-honored way of such Pecksniffs—made sure to load his book with graphic depictions of violence, such as the highly educational illustration of an Indian massacre reprinted on the next page.)

Even P. T. Barnum—who grew rich by assembling a museumful of dubious displays, from grotesquely deformed human "curiosities" to waxworks dioramas of grisly murders—was given to boasting about the "clean, pure, moral, and instructive" nature of his shows. "Never

cater to the baser instincts," he preached to his partner in 1891. "Strive as I have always done to elevate the moral tone of amusements, and always remember that children have ever been our best patrons. I am prouder of my title 'The Children's Friend' than if I were to be called 'The King of the World'."

Over the years, efforts have been made to market sanitized varieties of pop entertainments, clean-scrubbed versions of innately scruffy genres, from Biblical comic books to born-again Christian rock. During the Victorian era, high-minded publishers tried to counteract the evil influences of the penny dreadfuls by publishing so-called "penny healthfuls"—wholesome pulp fiction for the young.

Thanks to the miracle of modern technology, a new and controversial form of this phenomenon has recently appeared on the scene. Companies with names like MovieMask and CleanFlicks have begun offering digitally altered videos of theatrical films, purged of all offending bloodshed. The movies in question, moreover, are not low-budget shockers but lavishly produced, often award-winning, "prestige pictures" like *Braveheart* and *Saving Private Ryan*. Sensitive viewers can

Blame it on the Bayeux Tapestry

•

It's lucky for art lovers that companies like CleanFlicks—self-appointed censors in the business of cutting out the gory parts from popular entertainments—didn't exist in the Middle Ages. Otherwise, the Bayeux Tapestry—one the world's great visual masterpieces—might have had much of its imagery trimmed away so as not to offend medieval viewers.

Measuring 230 feet in length, this marvel of eleventh-century embroidery is not really a tapestry at all but rather an enormously long, narrow strip of linen depicting Willam the Conqueror's invasion of England in a string of fifty-eight sequential scenes. Back when it was new, it was hung around the nave of the local cathedral; to get the full impact, audiences made a circuit of the church, viewing the unfolding narrative one episode at a time.

Anyone lucky enough to visit northwestern France nowadays and see the Bayeux Tapestry up close is bound to be struck by the glorious handiwork that went into its creation. But there's something else that's striking about it: its resemblance to a modern day adventure film. Both in the way the story unfurls and in its vivid, kinetic details, there is something extremely cinematic about it. It is, in fact, a kind of proto-movie—a medieval *Saving Private Ryan,* portraying a cross-channel invasion followed by a monumental battle that changed the course of Western history.

The resemblance to Spielberg's film is amplified by the tapestry's exceptionally graphic depiction of violence. For all its beauty, it is filled with grisly images of death and mutilation, portraying the grim facts of medieval warfare with uncompromising realism. We see soldiers with their arms lopped off, their heads split open by broadswords, their guts spilling out of their bellies. There are men impaled by lances or pierced through the eye with arrows or trampled underfoot by horses. Indeed, this magnificent specimen of medieval craftsmanship is far gorier than most R-rated movies (a fact that was wittily acknowledged a few years back in a clever little magazine cartoon. Lying on a body-strewn battleground, one mortally wounded medieval soldier looks

(continued)

over at another and says: "I blame it all on the kids watching too much Bayeux Tapestry").

Besides being a wonderful aesthetic experience, viewing the Bayeux Tapestry is also an educational one, and among the lessons it teaches is that people have always craved violent, action-packed stories delivered in visual terms. Those who attack the American public for its supposed obsession with cinematic bloodshed are missing the point. Clearly, human beings have always thrilled to certain kinds of violent narratives and have constantly sought new and more exciting ways of bringing them to life. Back in 1077, when the Bayeux Tapestry was created, embroidery was state-of-the-art picture-making, and to create a moving image the audience had to do the moving.

In short, very little has changed in the past thousand years except for technology. Certainly human nature hasn't. Heroic action, sweeping adventure, and lots of graphic violence are the same crowd-pleasing ingredients as always. In effect, all we've really done in the last thousand years is find a way to endow the Bayeux Tapestry with motion, so that we can sit comfortably in our seats and watch the carnage take place before our eyes.

now enjoy a noisy but essentially bloodless reenactment of D-Day and watch scenes of ferocious thirteenth-century combat without seeing anyone actually get hurt.

The demand for these bowdlerized videos springs from a widely shared sense that today's Hollywood movies contain toxic levels of gore in comparison to the tasteful entertainments of the past. People seem to believe that gratuitous violence was invented by the likes of Wes Craven and Quentin Tarantino—unprincipled filmmakers who couldn't care less about the moral health of the Republic as long as their movies sell tickets. That this is received wisdom among a significant chunk of the citizenry doesn't, of course, mean that it is true. In point of fact, there's nothing new about extravagant violence in dramatic entertainment, and there have been times in the past when such make-believe mayhem was far more outrageous than anything in *Pulp Fiction* or *Scream*.

Back in the Middle Ages, for example, daily life was steeped in grotesque forms of violence. Public executions were such a crowd-pleasing spectacle that (as Barbara Tuchman notes in her 1978 best-seller, *A Distant Mirror*) the citizens of one French village, Mons, purchased a condemned criminal from a neighboring town "so that they should have the pleasure of seeing him quartered."[1] Animals were not only butchered for food but tortured for fun (Andrew McCall describes a popular sport in which men nailed a cat to a post, then competed to see who could be the first to batter it to death with his head).[2] And then there were the ubiquitous tales of martyred saints, whose hideous torments were graphically portrayed in pictures and words. Church paintings and stained glass windows showed them raising up their severed, dripping body parts for display; while books like Jacobus de Viragine's *The Golden Legend*—the most widely read work in medieval times after the Bible—described their tortures in the most excruciating imaginable detail. Here, for example, is the opening paragraph of Viragine's inspiring tale of Saint Quentin:

> Quentin, noble by birth and a Roman citizen, went to the city of Amiens and performed many miracles there. By order of Maximus, prefect of the city, he was taken prisoner and beaten until the executioners fainted from their exertions. Then he was jailed, but an angel set him free, and he went to the center of the city and preached to the people. Arrested again, he was stretched on the rack until his veins burst, then was whipped with raw thongs, then had boiling oil, pitch, and grease poured over his wounds. All these he bore patiently, meanwhile mocking the judge, who resented this and gave orders to force lime, vinegar, and mustard into his mouth. Even this did not move him, and he was taken to Veromandum. There the judge had two nails pounded into his body from head to legs, and ten pegs driven under his fingernails. Finally he was beheaded.[3]

Their manners may have been crude, but in the area of ghastly violence medieval peasants were clearly connoisseurs, who appreciated nothing better than a nicely performed quartering, disemboweling, or beheading. It is no surprise, then, that their theatrical productions were filled with elaborate depitions of violence. In England, the most popular stage works of the period were religious dramas known as "miracle plays" in which—as the scholar John Spalding Gatton has written—"the Apostles were graphically stoned, stabbed, blinded, crucified, and flayed. Other holy men and women variously and vigorously had their teeth wrenched out, their breasts torn off, and their bodies scourged, shot with arrows, baked, grilled and burned. Audiences were also treated to bestial scenes of infanticide, and to broad comedies about divinely mutilated Jews."[4]

Gatton's observation comes from his article, "There Must Be Blood"—a title taken from a stage direction in a fifteenth-century play, whose author clearly recognized that, whatever else it supplied in the way of entertainment and edification, a successful medieval drama required a profusion of gore to satisfy the audience. Gatton's article offers an eye-opening view not only of the sheer quantity of sickening violence in the religious dramas of the Middle Ages but of the highly realistic tricks used to simulate the bloodshed. In their grisly ingenuity, the special effects used by medieval stage technicians rivaled anything in an *Evil Dead* or a *Friday the 13th* movie. Indeed, Gatton's research makes it clear that—"in the name of sacred instruction"—English miracle plays and their French counterparts, the *mystères,* were nothing so much as a form of theatrical splatter entertainment.

One of the most popular motifs in medieval religious drama, for example, was the Slaughter of the Innocents—King Herod's attempt to eliminate the Christ Child by ordering the murder of all male infants under the age of two. In the various versions of this Biblical episode enacted on the English stage, babies were stabbed, hacked, impaled, dismembered, bisected, and beheaded. These atrocities were achieved with lifelike dolls equipped with detachable heads, cloth bodies, and concealed bladders that spurted fake blood all over the stage when punctured.

Another ancient episode—the destruction of Jerusalem by Titus in A.D. 70—provided a pretext for an even grislier dramatization of child slaughter. In the fifteenth-century French play, *The Vengeance of Our Lord,* a group of desperate mothers reluctantly conclude that the only way to stave off starvation is by devouring their own infants. Since the mere suggestion of cannibalistic infanticide was clearly insufficient for medieval theatergoers, technicians devised realistic dolls with removable limbs made of dough, so that the mothers could actually be shown feasting on the arms and legs of their children.

Besides repellent (if spiritually improving) scenes of baby slaughter, the hideous torture of women was a favorite theme of religious plays in the Middle Ages. One of the most popular female subjects was St. Barbara, whose martyrdom involved, among other horrible mutilations, the amputation of her breasts. Needless to say, medieval audiences insisted on seeing this atrocity enacted before their eyes. Gatton describes the ingenious means by which this ghastly piece of stage business was evidently achieved:

> Women's roles were often taken by men, a convention which would facilitate the "mutilation." In a performance of *The Life and Passion of St. Barbara* given at Metz in 1485, the heroine was played by a young barber's assistant named Lyonard, whom the *Chronicles* of the

city described as "very handsome" and resembling a "beautiful young girl"; he acted the role "so thoughtfully and reverently that several people wept for pity." He could have attached to his chest breasts made of cardboard or a form of papier-mâché which, when "amputated," would have likely revealed made-up areas of his skin simulating torn flesh, while effectively concealing his own nipples.

The French were especially inventive in creating horrific illusions, relying on skilled craftsman known as *Mâitres des Feints*—Masters of Special Effects. In one fifteenth-century *mystèrem, The Acts of the Apostles,* the audience was treated to the sight of nine separate beheadings, accomplished with life-size dummies painted to resemble the actors. Other characters were stoned with painted-sponge rocks, gutted with trick knives, scourged with fake whips, and clubbed with imitation cudgels.

Certain onstage tortures required more elaborate effects. A lifelike mannequin covered with strips of cloth "skin" was used for the flaying of St. Bartholomew; while the blinding of St. Matthew was performed with a particularly cunning contrivance: a fake augur that looked as if it were boring into the actor's eye sockets and extracting the orbs.

No celebration of Christian martyrdom would be complete without at least one fiery immolation—a requirement satisfied in *The Acts of the Apostles* by the burning of St. Barnabas. For added verisimilitude, the stand-in dummy was stuffed with animal entrails. As the figure blazed, the offal spilled onto the stage. By this clever means, as Gatton writes, "the stench of roasting flesh complement[ed] the sight of the body being consumed by the flame."

By Shakespeare's time, miracle plays had vanished from the English stage. Graphic gore and grotesque violence, however, remained as popular as ever. The Bard's own plays are packed with crowd-pleasing episodes of murder and mayhem, from the assorted homicides in *Hamlet* to the mounting carnage in *Macbeth* to such barely watchable scenes of sadistic cruelty as Gloucester's blinding in *King Lear* and the mutilation of Lavinia in *Titus Andronicus.* Even so, the violence in

Shakespeare's plays is positively restrained compared to the extravagant horrors dished out by other Elizabethan playwrights who specialized in the popular genre known as the "revenge tragedy."

The main influence on this extravagantly gruesome form of drama was the Roman tragedian, Seneca, whose plays not only dwelt on unspeakable acts of violence and cruelty but described them in minute detail. In Seneca's version of *Oedipus,* for example, the doomed king doesn't merely blind himself. Rather—as reported by a messenger—

> With a groan,
> A terrifying roar, he thrust his fingers
> Into his eyes; and those wild orbs stared out
> And seemed to rush to meet the hands they knew
> And to obey their summons, offering
> Themselves to their own fate. The fingers bent
> And groped in haste to find the seeing eyes,
> Then wrenched them from their roots and tore them out.
> And still the fingers probed the open holes,
> The nails scratched in the empty cavities
> Which now gaped hollow where the eyes had been.

When Hippolytus is killed in a chariot accident, we are given every dreadful particular of the event:

> The speeding wheels trundled the dying body
> Until it caught upon a half-burnt tree-stump,
> Sharp as a stake, which pierced the groin and held him
> Transfixed; and while the man hung there impaled,
> The car stood still, the horses at a loss,
> Checked by the accident. Then they break loose,
> Even though they break their master. Now half dead
> His flesh is ripped by brambles, gored by spines
> Of thorny thickets, broken into pieces
> Hanging on every tree.

And when Atreus slaughters and roasts his brother's children, a witness offers an account that (as one scholar puts it) amounts to a virtual recipe for the preparation of a human flesh banquet:[5]

> The entrails torn from the warm bodies lay
> Quivering, veins still throbbing, shocked hearts beating.
> Atreus picked at the pieces, scrutinized
> The message of the Fates, noted the signs
> In the internal organs hot with blood.
> Finding no blemish in the sacrifice
> He was content, and ready to prepare
> The banquet for his brother; hacked the bodies
> Limb from limb—detached the outstretched arms
> Close to the shoulders—severed the ligaments
> That tie the elbow joints—stripped every part
> And roughly wrenched each separate bone away—
> All this he did himself; only the faces,
> And trusting suppliant hands, he left intact.
> And soon the meat is on the spits, the fat
> Drips over a slow fire, while other parts
> Are tossed to boil in singing copper pans.[6]

However extreme, the horror in Seneca's plays was somewhat mitigated by the fact that it generally occurred offstage and was described after the fact. The audience heard about the atrocities but rarely witnessed them. Elizabethan dramatists like Cyril Tourneur, Thomas Drue, and Henry Chettle went Seneca one better, depicting every conceivable kind of inhuman cruelty in loving detail. In plays like *The Bloody Banquet, The Fatal Dowry, The Unnatural Combat, The Triumph of Death,* and *All's Lost by Lust,* characters are flayed alive, cooked in boiling oil, and dispatched with white-hot pokers shoved up their rectums. Slanderers have their tongues ripped out, wicked kings have their brains seared with burning crowns, bloodthirsty killers are forced to devour the flesh of their own butchered children. It is little wonder that disapproving modern critics have condemned the entire genre of the Elizabethan revenge tragedy for what one of them calls its "indiscriminate wading in blood."[7]

Some latterday scholars have made labored attempts to ascribe allegorical meanings to all the torture, murder, and dismemberment that filled these plays. Most agree however, that the gore was strictly gratuitous, serving no higher purpose than to provide morbid titillation to an audience that regarded public executions and bear-baiting as acceptable entertainments. As one early commentator put it, the whole point of such drama was to supply "a thrill which puts the spectator beside himself."[8]

To keep their customers satisfied, Elizabethan playwrights were constantly inventing new and more baroque forms of depravity. It wasn't enough for a drunken king to prove his skills by shooting an arrow through the breast of a six-year-old boy. The child's reeking heart had to be cut from his body and presented onstage to his grieving parent. The violence was so over the top that it sometimes reached ludicrous extremes. John Mason's 1608 revenge tragedy *The Turk* is prefaced with a synopsis (or "argument") that sums up the action: "*Timoclea,* finding the *Turk* enamored of *Amada,* kills her own daughter. *Borgias,* after many cunning tragical changes, strangles his wife with her own hair, stabs *Ferrara,* being in the shape of a eunuch. In the end, *Mulleasses* and *Borgias* kill one another, and the Duke of Venice, surviving all their black and treacherous plots, marries *Julia.*" It sounds like something dreamed up by Thomas Pynchon—who, in fact, includes a hilarious parody of revenge tragedies in his 1966 satirical masterpiece, *The Crying of Lot 49*.

A typical example of this outlandishly violent genre is John Marston's *Antonio's Revenge*. The play opens with the entrance of the evil Venetian duke, Piero Sforza, "his arms bare, smear'd in blood, a poniard in one hand, bloody." "Bursting forth in braggart passion," Piero proceeds to boast at length about his latest acts of "topless villainy." He has just poisoned his hated rival, the noble duke Andrugio. Then—to sabotage the wedding plans of his own daughter, Mellida, who is engaged to Andrugio's son, Antonio—Piero has stabbed to death a young nobleman named Feliche and placed the blood-drenched body beside the girl's sleeping form. The discovery of the young man's corpse in Mellida's bed will raise grave doubts about her chastity and put a serious damper on her wedding day.

Piero is so proud of having contrived these atrocities that he can't stop praising himself, proclaiming that he is "great in blood/Un-equal'd in vengeance." His gloating reaches new heights of rhetorical excess when he brags, in one especially revolting metaphor, that "I have been nurs'd in blood, and still have suck'd/ the steam of reeking gore!"

His crowning villainy is still to come. His scheme is to marry Andrugio's widow, then kill her son, Antonio. Anticipating this ultimate depravity, Piero is almost beside himself with glee. "By this warm, reeking gore, I'll marry her," he crows. "Poison the father, butcher the son, and marry the mother; ha!"

His plans are thwarted, however, when Andrugio's ghost rises from the grave and informs Antonio of Piero's nefarious deeds. Vowing to "suck red vengeance/Out of Piero's wounds," Antonio proceeds to stab the villain's young son, Julio, while crying out to the night: "Behold I spurt warm blood in thy black eyes!" He then sprinkles the little boy's blood over Andrugio's grave (or, as he so poetically puts it, "dews" the ground "with these fresh-reeking drops").

Far from allaying Antonio's appetite for vengeance, the murder of little Julio only whets it. "Lo, thus I heave my blood-dyed hands to heaven," he proclaims. "Even like insatiate hell, still crying: More!/ My heart hath thirsting dropsies after gore."

Since no self-respecting hero of an Elizabethan revenge tragedy would slay a villain's child without turning the tender flesh into a meat pie and then dishing it up to the father, the climax of the play is somewhat predictable. Marston provides an added soupçon of sadism by having Antonio rip out Piero's tongue before revealing the cannibal pasty. Only then is Piero put to death, stabbed repeatedly by Antonio and his confederates while Andrugio's ghost looks on in satisfaction and praises his son's actions: "'Tis done; and now my soul shall sleep in rest./Sons that revenge their father's blood are blest."

To make all these grisly goings-on seem as real as possible, Elizabethan stage technicians relied on the same gruesome effects pioneered by their medieval predecessors: phony heads that could be decapitated from dummies and impaled on pikes; fake skin that could be flayed from an actor's torso; concealed bladders filled with animal blood that could produce a satisfying spurt of gore when punctured.

Sometimes, the simplest tricks were the most effective. At the climax of Thomas Kyd's *The Spanish Tragedy,* for example, the hero, Hieronimo, bites off his own tongue to keep from confessing a secret. This ghastly piece of stage business was achieved with a chunk of calf's liver which the actor kept concealed in his mouth. At the appropriate moment, he pretended to bite down hard, then spat the bloody meat onto the boards (or, for even greater effect, into the audience).

The branch of stagecraft concerned with devising ingeniously gruesome special effects reached a kind of creative peak in turn-of-the-century Paris with the founding of a small playhouse whose productions were so outrageously violent that its name has become a byword for gratuitous gore: the Théâtre du Grand-Guignol.

The Grand-Guignol was the brainchild of a man named Oscar Métenier, a former police clerk, tabloid journalist, and playwright, whose work was rooted in literary naturalism, a movement that sought to expose the grim realities of lower-class life so blithely ignored by the smug bourgeoisie. The building he bought for this purpose in 1897 was a tiny, 285-seat theater on the Rue Chaptal that—ironically enough—had once been the chapel of a convent. In that bizarrely incongruous setting—where carved wooden angels hovered over the orchestra and the loges resembled confessionals—Métenier and his collaborators proceeded to mount works that stirred up outrage and controversy by dealing with the kinds of low-life characters that had never been portrayed on the Parisian stage: prostitutes, pimps, petty criminals, and so on.

"The Punch and Judy Show": Grand Guignol for Kids

•

Since the phrase "Grand Guignol" has become synonymous with outlandishly violent entertainment, it's surprising to learn what the term really means. It refers, of all things, to a puppet show. "Guignol" was the name of a popular French puppet, a wise-cracking mischief-maker with a flagrant contempt for authority. Since Oscar Méténier, the founder of the theater, was a social satirist whose goal was to outrage bourgeois sensibilities, he chose the impudent puppet as a suitably subversive mascot. In effect, Méténier was staging Guignol shows for grownups.

Besides a caustic tongue, Guignol possessed another characteristic that made him an apt symbol for Méténier's enterprise—a propensity for violence (he expressed his antiauthoritarian attitude, for example, by bludgeoning policemen). Nowadays, people associate puppets with such cute and cuddly creatures as Kermit the Frog. In the old days, however, many puppet shows featured an astonishing degree of brutal slapstick. This was particularly true of the most famous puppet of the Victorian age, Guignol's British counterpart, Mr. Punch of the wildly popular "The Punch and Judy Show."

In contrast to another favorite of nineteenth-century English audiences—a dimwitted marionette named Tim Bobbin—Punch was a hand puppet, a fact that helped account for his unbridled behavior. While marionettes are capable of certain forms of aggression—sword-fighting, for example—they can't overdo themselves when it comes to violent movements. As anyone who has seen Walt Disney's *Pinocchio* knows, a marionette that tries anything too rambunctious will quickly find himself tangled up in his own strings. Hand puppets, however, are perfectly designed for crude action. And Punch took full advantage of that ability. With the possible exception of "Itchy and Scratchy"—the insanely bloody cartoon that is Bart Simpson's favorite television program—there is nothing in the realm of contemporary kiddie

(continued)

entertainment as remotely violent as this centuries-old puppet show. Indeed, if Bart had been born during the reign of Queen Victoria, he would have spent his afternoons, not in front of the TV, but gathered with his cronies around an outdoor puppet booth, guffawing over the riotous antics of the irrepressibly brutal Punch.

The most famous account of a *Punch and Judy* show dates from 1827, when the journalist John Payne Collier and the artist George Cruikshank recorded a private performance by the famed Italian puppeteer Giovanni Piccini. The resulting text and illustrations were published in a book entitled, *The Tragical Comedy or Comical Tragedy of Punch and Judy.* The plot—which rises to the same level of comic sophistication as the average *Three Stooges* short—is nothing but a string of uproariously violent encounters. It begins when Punch goes to pet his neighbor's dog, which promptly clamps its teeth around the puppet's grotesquely oversized nose. After prying the dog loose, Punch summons the owner, Scaramouche and, after a bit of crude banter, knocks the fel-

low's head "clean off his shoulders." Punch then calls for his wife Judy and requests a kiss. She responds by walloping him in the face. Seeking another outlet for his affection, Punch asks for his infant child and begins to cradle it. Unfortunately, the baby picks that moment to dirty itself. Always the loving family man, Punch reacts by beating the baby's head against the stage, then hurling its dead body into the audience. When Judy reappears and discovers what's happened, she is understandably upset. Tearing Punch's stick from his hands, she begins to lay into him. He wrestles the cudgel away from her, pummels her to death, then breaks into a triumphant little song:

(continued)

> *Who'd be plagued with a wife*
> *That could set himself free*
> *With a rope or a knife*
> *Or a good stick, like me?*

The rest of the show consists of more the same. After being thrown from a horse while pursuing a nubile young woman Punch breaks his leg and kills the doctor who comes to treat him. In rapid succession, he then beats to death a black servant, a blind beggar, and a constable. Sentenced to death for his crimes, he tricks the executioner into slipping on the noose and manages to hang the hangman. In the end, he even slays the Devil himself, impaling "Old Nick" on his own trident.

Much has been written about the deeper sociopolitical significance of Punch and Judy. But—as the pop culture scholar James Twitchell has written—"although the *Punch* show is rich in political, social, and religious overtones, its one overwhelming characteristic is its ceaseless dedication to preposterous violence."

However shocking in their depiction of the seamy underbelly of French society, the plays mounted during Méténier's tenure paled by comparison to those staged by his successor, Max Maurey, who took over the management in 1897. It was Maurey who concocted the gruesome formula that would make the Grand-Guignol a theatrical sensation, replacing Méténier's raw social realism with outrageously gory melodrama: "slice-of-death" drama (as one wag put it) instead of slice-of-life. A natural showman with a flair for Barnumesque publicity stunts, Maurey advertised his showplace as "The House of Horrors" and took out newspaper ads showing patrons getting heart checkups before entering the theater. He also hired a house physician to revive any customers who collapsed from shock. According to legend, when a woman passed out during the doctor's first night on the job, he was unable to help her because he had passed out, too.

And, in fact, the shows staged at the Théâtre du Grand-Guignol were not for the faint of heart or weak of stomach. To be sure, comedic skits were a standard feature of the repertoire—broad, often risqué sketches with titles like *Adèle est grosse* (*Adèle is Fat*) and

Hue! Cocotte! (*Hey Cocotte!*). But these farcical playlets were offered solely as a respite from the main attractions. What drew the crowds to Maurey's "House of Horrors" weren't the spicy little sex romps but the insanely violent melodramas— harrowing spectacles of torture, murder, and horrendous mutilation. For the next half century, the tiny one-time chapel attracted untold numbers of respectable Parisians and well-heeled tourists seeking the ultimate in morbid titillation—graphic hardcore sadism of a kind that is impossible to witness nowadays outside the realm of the most repellent "video nasties" (as the British call such low-grade gore movies as *Zombie Flesh Eaters* and *Cannibal Holocaust*).

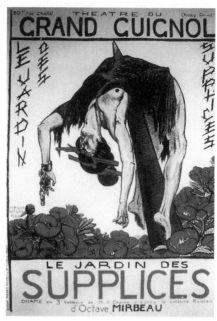

Those in search of gruesome thrills weren't disappointed. If anything, they generally got more than they bargained for. In plays like *The Garden of Torture, The Merchant of Corpses, The Kiss of Blood, The Castle of Slow Death, The Horrible Experiment,* and hundreds more, characters had their limbs graphically amputated, their eyes gouged out with every variety of implement, their skulls sawed open, their faces grilled on red-hot stoves or disfigured with sulfuric acid, their tongues ripped out, their entrails slowly yanked from their bellies. Audience members passed out with alarming regularity (Maurey is said to have judged the success of a play by the number of faintings it produced). Many of the productions induced even more violent reactions. It was not unusual for customers to bolt from the theater in the middle of a performance and vomit in the alley.

The plots, often full of cruelly ironic twists, were designed to reinforce the shocks. In *The Final Torture,* for example—one of the most famous and frequently performed of the Grand-Guignol plays—a French marine stationed outside Peking during the Boxer Rebellion has his hands cut off by the Chinese. Making his way back to his besieged embassy, he displays his mutilated stumps to the head consul, D'Hemelin, and—with his dying breath—describes the unspeakable atrocities being perpetrated against foreigners. To spare his daughter a fate worse than death, D'Hemelin, shoots her in the head—only to be rescued by Allied forces, who burst into the embassy seconds after the unfortunate diplomat executes his beloved child. D'Hemelin promptly goes insane.

The greatest of all the Grand-Guignol stars was a glamorous actress named Maxa. During her celebrated career as "the most assassinated woman in the world" (as she was proudly billed), Maxa

was subjected to a range of tortures unique in theatrical history: she was shot with a rifle and with a revolver, scalped, strangled, disemboweled, raped, guillotined, hanged, quartered, burned, cut apart with surgical tools and lancets, cut into eighty-three pieces by an invisible Spanish dagger, stung by a scorpion, poisoned with arsenic, devoured by a puma, strangled by a pearl necklace, and whipped; she was also kissed by a leper and subjected to a very unusual metamorphosis, which was described by one theater critic: "Two hundred nights in a row, she simply decomposed on stage in front of an audience. The operation lasted a good two minutes during which the young woman transformed little by little into an abominable corpse."

These and the countless other atrocities carried out on the stage of the Grand-Guignol were performed with the aid of exceptionally convincing stage tricks. The most famous gimmick was the fake blood, of which untold gallons were spilled in the course of the theater's sixty-year history. Based on a closely guarded recipe, the blood came in nine different shades and coagulated as it dried, forming convincing scabs on the flesh of the players. Disemboweled entrails were fashioned from red rubber hoses; amputated hands from glue-stiffened gloves; flayed skin from strips of painted adhesive plaster.

Various techniques were used for the frequent gouging of eyes. Some stage directors relied on actual sheep's eyeballs, which produced a satisfyingly squishy effect when punctured with a knitting needle or scooped out with a spoon. Others preferred taxidermical eyes, which gave a nice theatrical bounce when they hit the stage. The drama historian Mel Gordon describes some of the other favorite tricks used at the Grand-Guignol:

> Daggers with retractable blades spurted blood when the blood-filled handles were squeezed. Dying victims could reveal throat and facial wounds by tracing their blood-soaked fingers over the imagined areas. Sword- or knife-wielding murderers could seemingly penetrate their victims' limbs by using a stage weapon with an empty curved clasp between the handle and blade. Out of nowhere, lunatics could suddenly foam at the mouth simply by chewing on a hidden bit of soap. Mirrors, facial masks, concealed rubber pieces for wounds and burns, fake heads and limbs, all the paraphernalia of magicians, when expertly used—during moments of darkness or out of the spectators' view—created an atmosphere of sickening and eerie realism.[9]

The Théâtre du Grand-Guignol lasted until 1962, though by then it was long past its prime. Still, it continued to deliver the shocking goods right until the very end. On the occasion of its closing, *Time* magazine paid tribute to the hideous delights the Grand-Guignol had dished out for so long:

> The last clotted eyeball has plopped onto the stage. The last entrail has been pulled like an earthworm from a conscious victim. . . . Only recently audiences watched a nude and lissome actress nailed to a cross and carved to pieces by a group of gypsy magicians

chanting something that sounded like a Protestant hymn sung backwards. Still another victim was bound, gagged, and whipped; then the tips of her breasts were clipped off with hedge shears and her eyes were scooped out with a soup spoon and a jackknife.

"We are very proud of that sequence," said Charles Nonon, the Grand Guignol's last director. "We consider it very original."[10]

Glorying in the most appallingly sadistic behavior imaginable, the blood-drenched melodramas of the Grand-Guignol offered vivid testimony to the atavistic appetites that persist in the civilized soul—to our age-old hunger for spectacles of suffering, torture, and violent death. In that sense, they can be viewed as depressing proof of our abidingly primitive nature.

Looked at from a different angle, however, they can be seen in a far more positive light—as a sign of how much progress we've made in devising clever ways to satisfy those dark primal urges. After all, even the most grisly productions in the Grand-Guignol's repertoire were only make-believe. No one really got hurt. And—apart from the audience members who passed out from fright or had to dash from the theater before losing their dinners—everyone had a good time.

SIX

•

*So you want to know where our festivals are held? The grape
harvests, Shrovetide frolics, and other events which are celebrated by country folk in your sunny land with wine, dancing, and general merrymaking? Well, I will tell you. They are
held at Newgate, sir, if there happens to be an execution, or
in Horsemonger Lane, or at some other nice place outside the
jails. Crowds of people assemble there from daybreak until
the moment when the hangman performs his horrible duty.
Your fairs and festivals are sparsely attended as compared
with the multitudes who assemble at these places. The windows of the surrounding houses are let at high prices; stands
for spectators are erected; stalls for the sale of food and drink
spring up in the vicinity like mushrooms. The people pay
good prices for beer and brandy. People come along from great
distances on foot and on horseback, or in carriages, to witness
the barbarous performance. And the first rows are occupied by
women, by my countrywomen. But they are by no means
women of the lower classes only. They also include smartly
dressed ladies, pretty girls with golden locks.*

—LETTER FROM A VICTORIAN WOMAN TO
A GERMAN VISITOR TO ENGLAND, 1852

Back in 1305, the Scottish hero William Wallace was captured by the
English, condemned as a traitor, and slowly put to death in a field outside the city walls of London. Before an excited crowd of spectators—
who comported themselves as if they were attending a thrilling
theatrical performance—Wallace was first hanged until he began to

lose consciousness, then cut down from the scaffold. After he revived, his genitals were sliced off and cast into a fire. Next, his abdomen was opened and his entrails pulled out and burned before his eyes. Only then was he put to death by decapitation. Afterwards, his body was dismembered and dipped into boiling tar. The various pieces were then put on public display around the city—his head at London Bridge, his right arm on the bridge at Newcastle-upon-Tyne, his left arm at Berwick, his right leg at Perth, and his left leg at Aberdeen.

Nearly seven centuries later—in the summer of 1995—this scene was reenacted in multiplex theaters around the nation at the conclusion of the hit movie, *Braveheart*. Only this time the execution was a highly tasteful affair. The hero (played by Mel Gibson) was briefly strung up by his wrists and ankles in a manner that showed off his muscles to handsome advantage. Then he was quickly dispatched in a way that the viewer never so much as glimpsed.

Clearly, there is both good and bad news here. The bad news is that audiences apparently still enjoy watching other people die in horrible ways. The good news is that we are willing to settle for simulations— and relatively tame ones at that.

Of course, there are idealists who would feel much better if people abjured violent entertainment altogether. Sadly, we are members of a murderous species, and our "primordial instinct for bloodshed and cruelty" (in Erwin Panofsky's phrase) continues to demand gratification. What we ought to take heart from is the *kind* of violence that fills our movie, TV, and video screens—which is to say, the fake kind. Computerized zombies that batten on human brains and cinematic psychos who carve up their victims with chainsaws might seem symptomatic of a culture in an advanced stage of decadence. But such make-believe mayhem is very benign indeed compared to the grisly spectacles of former times, when living, flesh-and-blood humans were subjected to unspeakable outrages for the delectation of the crowd.

To appreciate just how civilized we really are nowadays, it is only necessary to read the first few pages of Michel Foucalt's *Discipline and Punish,* a groundbreaking study of the development of the modern prison system, that begins with an account of the 1757 execution of Robert François Damiens for the attempted assassination of King Louis XV. Since the crime was considered so egregious, Damiens was condemned to a particularly horrific death. According to the sentence, he was to be conveyed in a cart to the Place de Grève, "where, on a scaffold that will be erected there, the flesh will be torn from his breasts, arms, thighs, and calves with red-hot pincers, his right hand, holding the knife with which he committed the said parricide, burnt with sulphur, and, on those places where the flesh will be torn away, poured molten lead, boiling oil, burning resin, wax and sulphur melted together and then his body drawn and quartered by four horses and his limbs and body consumed by fire, reduced to ashes and his ashes thrown to the winds."[1]

The full description of Damiens's torture occupies several pages in Foucalt's book, and (as the author no doubt intended) strikes the modern reader as appalling beyond belief. That we react with such horrified incredulity to the mere description of the victim's suffering is significant in itself, suggesting that—for all our exposure to virtual violence—we are actually quite sheltered from the real thing and have a very limited tolerance for it. Our popular culture may be saturated with synthetic gore, but at least we don't spend our leisure time watching real people have their eyes put out, their limbs pulverized, their sex organs amputated and their flesh torn to pieces with red-hot pincers.

People in earlier ages certainly did. For them, an execution was a festive occasion, made all the more enjoyable if they were treated to the sight of a particularly unusual and gruesome form of torture. When Richard Rouse—a cook in the the employ of John Fisher, Bishop of Rochester—was convicted of using poison yeast to murder several members of the cleric's family in 1531, authorities ordered that he be boiled alive—a punishment apparently regarded as especially apt for a cook. The sentence was carried out at Smithfield a few days later. "Because of its novelty," one historian has written, "the event attracted a far larger crowd than attended the more commonplace executions of hanging or burning."[2]

Animal Torture for Fun and Profit

•

Human beings aren't the only living creatures who have been tortured and killed for the amusement of the masses. For several millennia, the sadistic treatment of animals was a major source of popular entertainment.

In ancient Rome, the human carnage of the gladiatorial games was supplemented by barbaric spectacles known as *venationes*, or "hunts"—a highly misleading term, since, as historian Roland Auguet puts it, "they had nothing of the hunt about them." The main appeal of the *venationes* for the blood-hungry crowds was the chance to watch a bunch of animals being massacred in a variety of interesting ways. Sometimes, creatures of the same species—a pair of panthers or lions, for example—were pitted against each other in savage fights that only ended when one lay dead, at which point the mangled victor was killed by armed men. Even more exciting to the jaded crowds were the death matches involving exotic combinations of creatures: elephants vs. boars, bulls vs. pythons, lions vs. crocodiles—even bears vs. seals. Other so-called combats were nothing but displays of pure sadism, as when an entire pride of lions was set loose on a single deer, whose frenzied—and futile—efforts to escape destruction brought howls of amusement from the spectators. There were occasions in which the animals were slaughtered by men. Auguet describes one such event, staged by Pompey and involving a score of elephants and a troop of warriors from a nomadic tribe known as the Getuli:

The Getuli were skilled hunters and had a very specialized hunting technique: they threw their javelins, aiming at the lower eyelids, and the beasts, struck in the brain, collapsed on the spot before they could advance a step, to the great surprise of the spectators; or else they paralyzed them by piercing their feet. One of the elephants, thus transfixed by several javelins, dragged itself on its knees towards its adversaries and began to tear away their shields and throw them in the air. The public regarded this as a "stunt" and laughed.[3]

From the middle ages onward,

(continued)

people took great pleasure in "baiting" animals, especially bulls. Indeed, this activity was so popular in eighteenth-century England that, in certain villages, butchers were legally required to bait a bull before slaughtering it. This highly diverting pastime consisted of tethering a bull to a stake by a fifteen-foot rope, then siccing a bulldog on him. The dog did its best to clamp its eye teeth on the bull's muzzle, dewlaps, or testicles, while the bull tried to break the dog's neck by snagging it with a horn and flinging it thirty feet or so in the air.

Bear baiting was another favorite form of this "sport," though not as common as bull baiting, bears being harder to come by. A popular alternative was badger baiting. In this variation, a badger was chained to a stake by its tail and a bunch of dogs set on him. "The jaws and teeth of the badger being exceptionally strong," writes historian E. D. Cuming, "he might kill or maim half a dozen dogs before he succumbed himself."[4]

Badger baiting was a popular spectator sport in this country as late as the 1890s, as were matches pitting rats against dogs. An article published in the February 14, 1891, issue of the *Police Gazette* described a delightful evening at Charles Norton's popular resort in Newark, New Jersey, which drew sporting men from all over the New York metropolitan region:

At about 10 o'clock, the master of ceremonies, Dick Toner, announced that the act of rat extermination was about to begin. A white bull pup, introduced as "Tommy," was placed into the rat pit, which was ten feet square and nearly four feet high. Dick, with the aid of his pinchers, lifted from a cage a large, fat and juicy rat and dropped it into the enclosure. At first the pup showed signs of friendliness, but his ratship was of not so social a disposition, but more of the pugilistic order. Angered, "Tommy" gave him a nip which ended his young life. As "Tommy" proved himself a good ratter, five were placed in the pit, only to meet a speedy death. . . . The event of the evening was when Toner placed a brindle bitch in with fifteen of the rats, all of which were quickly given their quietus. On several occasions, the cornered victims would turn on the bitch

(continued)

and show fight, but the odds against them were too much and they soon had to give up the ghost. Prof. Norton has decided to make this popular sport a feature of his establishment, and will on each Tuesday evening give an exhibition.[5]

Of all forms of animal blood sport, cockfighting has been the most perennially popular. In England, all classes indulged in it, from aristocrats to the humblest villager. The birds were generally equipped with sharpened spurs, some shaped like sickles, others like penknives or needles. One eighteenth-century French observer described the sport this way:

The animals used are of a particular breed; they are large but short-legged birds, their feathers are scarce, and are very ugly to look at. . . . The stage on which they fight is round and small. One of the cocks is released, and struts about proudly for a few seconds. He is then caught up and his enemy appears. When the bets are made, one of the cocks is placed on either end of the stage; they are armed with silver spurs, and immediately rush at each other and fight furiously. It is surprising to see the ardour, the strength, and the courage of these little animals, for they rarely give up until one of them is dead. . . . The noise is terrible, and it is impossible to hear yourself speak unless you shout. . . . Cocks will sometimes fight a whole hour before one or the other is victorious.[6]

Even in recent times, purveyors of pop entertainment have thought nothing of inflicting severe, if not lethal, damage on animals for the amusement of audiences. For decades, makers of Hollywood westerns and other period adventure movies made use of hidden "trip wires" to bring galloping horses and their stunt riders crashing to the ground. Whenever John Wayne shot a pony out from underneath a charging Apache warrior, it was really a trip wire that brought the animal down. The resulting scenes were exciting for viewers—and frequently fatal to the horses, which were either killed outright from the violence of the spill or so badly crippled that they had to be destroyed.

Anyone who doubts that today's popular culture is more civilized and humane than that of past

(continued)

ages might consider the block-buster movie, *The Perfect Storm*. An adaptation of Sebastian Junger's bestseller about a Gloucester sword-fishing vessel lost during a hurricane of historical dimensions, the film features several scenes showing the crew catching and killing swordfish. At the very end of the film, this disclaimer appears:

"The American Humane Society monitored the animal action. No animal was harmed. Scenes appearing to place animals in jeopardy were simulated. No live fish were used in the making of this film."

In every preceding era of Western culture, people took unabashed pleasure in watching the torture and death of all sorts of animals—bulls, bears, dogs, cats, badgers, rodents, and roosters. Nowadays, we have evolved to the point where the public will not even tolerate gratuitous violence against a fish.

Breaking on the wheel was another form of barbarity that brought the crowds out in unusually high numbers. The most common form of this torture consisted of binding the felon to a large cartwheel. Using a three-foot iron bar or a sledgehammer, according to his preference, the executioner would proceed to pulverize each of the victim's limbs. During the Dark Ages, the shattered arms and legs of the still-living victim were threaded through the spokes, the wheel was attached to a wooden post and set up for display, and the victim was allowed to die in the most inconceivable agony.

In later centuries, thanks to the growing refinement of European sensibilities, letting a hideously mangled person perish slowly at a public crossroads while his eyes were pecked out by ravens was judged to be overly harsh, and criminals subjected to breaking were put out of their misery with a crushing blow to the stomach, throat, or heart—though the coup de grace was sometimes withheld for a few hours, depending on the severity of the crime.

There were several variations on the torture. Sometimes the victim was broken, not on a cartwheel, but on an *X*-shaped "St. Andrew's cross." And occasionally, both the wheel *and* the cross were employed to enhance the suffering of the felon and add to the overall interest of the spectacle. This was the case with the 1705 execution of Boéton de St.-Laurent d'Aigorse, a Huguenot condemned for plotting against the government. In his encyclopedic study of judicial torture methods, Geoffrey Abbott—former Yeoman Warder of the Tower of London—provides a vivid description of Boéton's ghastly end:

> Meanwhile, the scaffold had been erected on the Esplanade, and on it the St. Andrew's cross waited, its four arms having had hollows scooped in them so that only the elbow and knee joints of the victim's limbs would rest on the timber. This fearsome modification meant that the rest of his arm and leg bones were entirely unsupported, thereby allowing them to be more easily shattered. At one of the corners of the scaffold a small carriage wheel hung on a pivot, the upper edges of it having been cut in a serrated fashion resembling a saw. Upon this bed of agony the victim would be stretched after having had his limbs shattered, so that the spectators would be able to see his final convulsions.
>
> Boéton was taken to the Esplanade in a tumbril, surrounded by drummers so that his exhortations could not be heard. . . . As soon as he stepped on to the scaffold, he voluntarily stretched himself on the cross, but the executioner told him he must undress. Rising again, he allowed the assistant to remove his doublet and trousers. As he resumed his position on the cross, the assistant bound him tightly to its wooden arms.
>
> A grim silence fell over the crowd surrounding the scaffold as the executioner approached, holding a square iron bar about three feet long, an inch and a half square, with a rounded handle. On seeing it, Boéton started to sing a Psalm, but almost immediately interrupted it with a faint cry as the executioner broke the bones of his right leg.
>
> He resumed his singing, however, an instant later, and kept it up without stopping, although the executioner proceeded to break, one after the other, the right thigh, the other shin and thigh, and each arm in two places. He then detached from the cross the shape-

less, mutilated trunk, still living and singing the praises of God, and, picking it up, laid it on the small wheel, with the poor, mangled legs folded beneath the body, so that the heels were touching the back of the head. Through the whole atrocious performance the victim's weak and tremulous voice never for one instant ceased to sing the praises of the Lord.[7]

Boéton's performance—singing away even while his limbs were being turned to pulp—won the hearts of the audience. In appreciation of his pluck, he was allowed a relatively swift deliverance from his suffering, the executioner dispatching him with a single savage blow to the chest.

A good deal of ingenuity went into devising appropriate tortures for criminals, as the Dutch historian Pieter Spierenberg makes clear. In his book *The Spectacle of Suffering,* Spierenberg provides a chart detailing the creative forms of punishment meted out for various crimes in Holland between 1650–1750:

YEAR	CRIME	PUNISHMENT
1651	A man was discovered committing a burglary by a nightwatchman. He fled but was stopped by another. He stabbed this watchman, who died the next day.	His right hand was cut off, then he was hanged and his corpse exposed. The hand was—and remained—nailed to the pillory.

YEAR	CRIME	PUNISHMENT
1660	Because he wanted the other's money, a man killed an acquaintance by hitting him twice with an iron spade.	The hangman hit him on head twice with that very spade. Then the convict was garroted. His corpse was exposed with the spade standing beside it.
1661	A man of twenty-one had committed nineteen burglaries. He used to bind and threaten his victims.	His hand was cut off on a log. Then he was hanged.
1664	An eighteen-year-old girl killed her landlady with an axe.	The hangman gave her a few strokes with the same axe. Then she was garroted.
1668	A Norwegian servant girl set fire to the house of a friend's master.	She was first garroted. Then her face was scorched by fire.
1673	A Scotsman came to the Netherlands in order to burn Dutch ships for the English.	He was broken on the wheel. Then his face was scorched with a bundle of straw.
1699	A sailor tried to rob someone. He attempted to kill his victim with a cobblestone.	He was garroted. Before he was completely dead, the hangman gave him three blows on the head with the cobblestone.
1720	A woman owed money to another. She went to the latter's house and hit her three times on the head with a hammer.	She was first strangled until half dead. Then her head was smashed with the hammer. Garroting was completed after this.
1750	A woman murdered a servant girl and the latter's mistress. She cut the girl into pieces, which she dropped into different canals. She had robbed the other woman and wanted it to look as though the servant had done it.	She was broken on the wheel. Before she was dead the hangman cut her throat. Then her head was cut off and put on a stake. Her right hand and both lower legs were cut off and laid upon her body.[8]

Since many of the mutilations performed on these victims were inflicted after death, they were clearly carried out for the benefit of the audience—to impress them with the awful power of the State and to serve as a deterrent. Despite the grim intent, however, these "spectacles of suffering" were far from somber occasions. On the contrary, as all available records show, they tended to be highly festive, if not carnivalesque, affairs at which the spectators often comported themselves with all the gravity and decorum of a bunch of beer-soaked revelers at a hockey game.

The sheer number of people who came to gawk at the dying agonies of the condemned was staggering. In 1682, a mass auto-da-fé in the main square of Lisbon, at which twenty-one heretics were burned at the stake, drew twenty thousand people. A century later, in 1786, an equally massive crowd gathered before Newgate Prison to see a murderess named Phoebe Harris burned alive. Even run-of-the-mill hangings attracted hordes of eager spectators. No fewer than forty-five thousand men, women, and children turned out in February 1807 to watch a pair of English highwaymen, John Holloway and Owen Haggerty, go to the gallows.

The situation was no different in America. When a desperado named Henry Kriegler was hanged in Minnesota on a raw afternoon in March 1861, approximately ten thousand people showed up, despite the discouraging weather. Some had traveled up to fifty miles by wagon to see him dangle. The execution of nineteen-year-old James Moran in Philadelphia on May 19, 1837, drew twice as many people, partly because of the novelty of watching someone so young put to death. In comparison to such numbers, the crowd of six thousand that attended the hanging of William Jackson in Chicago in June 1837 seems almost meager. Still, from contemporary accounts, Jackson's execution was an enjoyable affair for everyone save the condemned. Vendors did a brisk business in lemonade, peanuts, and confections, fathers hoisted their children onto their shoulders to give the little ones a better view, and women, young and old, chattered gaily.

The fun sometimes extended beyond the felon's death. In his book,

The Lesson of the Scaffold, historian David Cooper describes a few eighteenth-century changes in British penal law that provided the public with additional opportunities to indulge their morbid voyeurism:

> In 1752, British legislators passed "An Act for the Better Preventing the Horrid Crime of Murder" in an attempt to deter murder by adding an additional "mark of infamy" to the punishment of death. The murderer's body was to be given over to surgeons for dissection, and to make this innovation consistent with executing publicly, the dissections were often carried out in public.
>
> The act also gave the the judge the discretion to order the body to be hanged in chains, so that it would remain suspended as a grisly warning. . . .
>
> Many a strip of green waste by the roadside and many a gorse-covered common had its gibbet, from which swung in the breeze the clanking and creaking iron hoops. There was gruesome aspect enough to a tar-saturated, deteriorating body, but to add to the degrading character of the penalty, gibbets were often placed near the

places of the crime and occasionally in front of the criminal's house. But they were always exposed to the public.

The day appointed for hanging in chains was a public event, and months later people would still gather around the gibbet.[9]

Given how much pleasure people derived from executions, it's no wonder that, as Cooper writes, the "mood could become ugly if the pleasure of viewing a hapless victim put to death were interfered with by the authorities." Cooper relates an anecdote about a barrister named Basel Montagu, who obtained a reprieve for two men sentenced to death for stealing sheep in 1801. The populace—which had been eagerly anticipating the hanging—was so incensed that "the High Sheriff of Huntingdon strongly advised [Montagu] to leave town as speedily as possible to avoid ill-treatment 'from the disappointment he had occasioned'."[10]

Ugly behavior was, in fact, a common feature of public executions. Attending his first hanging in 1846, Charles Dickens was appalled less by the punishment itself than by the attitude of the spectators. "No sorrow, no salutary horror, no abhorrence, no seriousness," he wrote. "Nothing but ribaldry, debauchery, levity, drunkenness, and flaunting vice in fifty other shapes." Pickpockets worked the crowd. So did prostitutes, who knew that—as has been true since the heyday of the Roman Coliseum—watching human beings suffer and die can have an aphrodisiac effect on certain people. Indeed, a grotesque air of lewdness suffused these supposedly grim proceedings. Dickens noted with disgust the crowd's "indecent delight when swooning women were dragged away by police with their dresses disordered."

At times the crowds grew so unruly that the area around the scaffold resembled a mosh pit. Drunken men "would knock off the hats of fellow spectators and roar as these were bounced back through the crowd," writes one historian. "They might even bounce along a spectator, with his legs in the air and his head down."[11] Fistfights would erupt as ruffians jockeyed for position at the foot of the gallows. When the hangman sprang the bolt and the victim plunged through the trap, spectators would whistle, cheer, and crack coarse jokes about the funny contortions of the dying man's limbs as he convulsed in the air.

Occasionally, the situation got seriously out of hand. In 1844, a dozen spectators were crushed to death at a Nottingham execution when a group of rowdies set off a panic in the crowd. Perhaps the worst of these incidents occurred at the Holloway–Haggerty double hanging in 1807. As David Cooper describes it, the scene was reminiscent of the kind of rioting that occasionally breaks out nowadays at soccer stadiums and rock arenas. "The pressure of the uncontrolled crowds, and the ensuing panic after many people tried forcefully to shove their way out, caused mass hysteria even before the criminals walked to the scaffold. People from behind, trying to escape the pressure, trampled over spectators in front. A fierce struggle broke out, everyone fighting to escape the crush. After the bodies were cut down, the marshals cleared the streets. There lay nearly one hundred persons on the street, either dead or unconscious."[12]

Though the criminal underworld and other members of the so-called "lower orders" always turned out in force for an execution, the audience was by no means composed entirely of ruffians, rowdies, prostitutes, and paupers, for whom a public hanging was a form of free entertainment, as well as a welcome diversion from the wretchedness of their daily lives. Attending a hanging at Newgate, the novelist William Thackery described "quiet fat family parties of simple honest tradesmen and their wives, looking on with the greatest imaginable calmness and sipping their tea." Certainly, there were enough reasonably well-off people at these events to fatten the wallets of the ballad mongers and food vendors. Like modernday fairgoers munching happily on cotton candy and corn dogs, the crowds at executions liked to gorge themselves on treats: hot potatoes, fruit, gingerbread cookies. Piemen always did a lively business—a fact that attested not only to the number of spectators with a little disposable income in their pockets, but to their holiday mood. As one historian puts it, the brisk sale of these comestibles clearly proves "how few stomachs were turned by the events."[13] Tavern keepers profited handsomely from the preexecution supper parties hosted by young men-about-town.

For a Victorian dandy, a public execution was a form of light entertainment and a good place to squire a date. As historian Thomas Laqueur writes:

A young man in nineteenth-century London might visit a coffee house for breakfast on a Sunday morning, walk to the Old Bailey to see how preparations for an execution were proceeding, have dinner, and then pick up his mistress for a walk over to Horsemonger Lane to check on how the construction of a scaffold for another hanging was coming along. The next day he might get up early to catch both events, commenting on how well the condemned behaved, remarking that he had never seen a woman hanged before, and that this was, as far as he could remember, the only occasion on which two people were hanged on the same day.[14]

The aristocracy showed up, too. Some arrived in coaches and picnicked from hampers as they watched the felons die. Others rented balcony seats from landlords with advantageous views. The cost of a room overlooking the scaffold wasn't cheap. "As late as the 1850s," according to Keith Hollingsworth, "a room with a good window still brought twenty guineas."[15] Like scalpers outside a sports stadium, landlords made their way through the crowd, offering the best seats in the house: "Comfortable rooms! Excellent situation! Beautiful prospect! Splendid view!"

For a smaller (though still exorbitant) sum, spectators who didn't want to mingle with the unwashed mob could rent a place on one of the wooden grandstands erected by enterprising types known as "Tyburn pew openers." The money that could be realized from these hastily built platforms was considerable. According to Geoffrey Abbott, one entrepreneur "reaped a profit of five hundred pounds" at the execution of an earl.[16] Still—though they were invariably advertised as sturdy and secure—these viewing stands carried risks of their own.

At the 1747 beheading of Lord Lovat—the last person publicly executed on Tower Hill—a scaffolding holding nearly nine thousand onlookers collapsed, killing a dozen people and injuring scores. Because of the hefty fees they charged—as much as three guineas for a spot on a dangerously overcrowded platform—the proprietors sometimes incurred the wrath of their customers. Abbott records the case of one "Mammy Douglas" who, in 1758, "increased the price of her stand seats for the hanging of Dr. Henesy, guilty of treason. Despite protests, the public, as usual, paid up, but their indignation turned to fury when, just as the hangman was about to execute the victim, a messenger arrived bearing a reprieve. A riot ensued, the stands were demolished by the mob, and the attempts to hang Mammy Douglas instead were narrowly averted."[17]

The Dissection Show

•

In November 2002, a German doctor named Gunther von Hagens provoked a storm of outrage when he performed a commercially televised autopsy in London. Before a paying crowd of four hundred people—and a home audience in the untold millions—von Hagens dissected the corpse of an unidentified 72-year-old German businessman who had given his consent for the public postmortem. Von Hagens claimed that he was simply reviving an old tradition, when autopsies were performed before the public, as portrayed in Rembrandt's famous painting, "The Anatomy Lesson of Dr. Nicholas Tulp," which shows the latter dissecting a cadaver before a rapt audience.

Von Hagens was already notorious for mounting a show called "Body Worlds," using actual human corpses preserved by his patented method of "plastination" and arranged in various poses—running, swimming, fencing, horseback riding. Even some who defended the "Body Worlds" exhibit, however, were sharply offended by the televised autopsy. In a scathing editorial, for example, *The New York Times* wrote that—

(continued)

contrary to his highfalutin claims—there was no historical precedent for his performance, since the general public had *never* been permitted to attend autopsies. Even in Dr. Tulp's day, declared the *Times,* they were open only to "fellow scientists and physicians."

Certainly, the editorial writers of *The New York Times* are entitled to their opinion. It's surprising, however, that the "newspaper of record"—which prides itself on its accuracy—was so wrong in this case. The fact is that, in the past, autopsies were *not* attended solely by specialists. Lay people came to watch, too. The resulting scenes were far from somber. On the contrary, they often turned quite rowdy.

According to the pathologist/essayist Dr. F. Gonzalez-Crussi, dissections became such a popular form of spectacle in Europe during the sixteenth century that "amphitheaters had to be built to accommodate the audience." Posters affixed to the columns of the building advertised the upcoming demonstration, which drew a colorful assortment of spectators:

Successful physicians, prominent members of the community, intellectuals, and the inevitable idle and rich snobs, apart from medical students, gathered in the amphitheater. This motley crowd generated no small commotion with gossip, bumptiousness, and self-display. Liveried lackeys appeared who circulated amidst the attendees distributing bouquets and oranges to the ladies, that the "perfume of the ones and the sweet aroma of the others" assist them in brooking the unpleasantness of the emanations wafting to their noses from the opened cadaver. Members of the aristocracy received sticks smeared with aromatic resins, which were to be burned during their performance as one more expedient against revolting odors.

In Bologna—where the amphitheater was "magnificently decorated for the occasion" with damask draperies and blazing candelabra—spectators initially had to pay for admission. When the fee was dropped in 1546, the crowds became even more heterogeneous—and unruly:

We may gather the increased confusion that resulted, since decrees were passed ordering

(continued)

guards to be posted at the doors to discourage the rowdiest and most troublesome spectators. Huge crowds thronged the place when Vesalius demonstrated the anatomy of the female genital system, and eager watchers jostled to get closer to the scene, to touch, indeed, the structures exposed.

It was the same throughout Europe, wherever public anatomical demonstrations took place. Historians tell us of professors in Germany who were compelled to sternly enjoin the spectators, especially during the dissection of female genital organs, to keep due decorum. In Holland, laws were promulgated that tried to check the inappropriate outbursts of persons who laughed, clapped, asked "indecent" questions, grabbed the specimens prepared by the dissector, or otherwise attempted to disrupt the solemnity of the occasion. But it was in Italy . . .

that the show assumed its flashiest, most striking and splendiferous features. It is of special significance that, in Bologna, dissections were performed during Carnival, beginning on the Feast of Saint Anthony (January 17). Accordingly, there was a festive character to the ceremony, and some persons came masked, or in carnivalesque disguise, to watch the proceedings.[18]

In short—like public executions—dissections of human corpses were yet another ghoulish form of entertainment: a "show," as Gonzalez-Crussi puts it. The only difference between Dr. von Hagen's televised autopsy and the anatomical demonstrations so popular in Renaissance Europe is that—thanks to the miracle of modern technology—viewers in 2002 could indulge their morbid curiosity from the comfort of home without having to stifle the stench with resin inhalers and oranges.

By the late 1800s, the sort of moral revulsion voiced by Charles Dickens had come to prevail in Western societies. To be sure, the occasional public execution continued to be carried out in some countries—including our own—until well into this century. (The last state-sanctioned public hanging in America took place, shockingly enough, as late as 1936, when a young black man, Rainey Bethea, was put to death before a cheering crowd of twenty thousand spectators in Owensboro, Kentucky.)

For the most part, however, this barbaric custom had been abolished by the turn of the century, depriving people of a form of titillating spectacle that had been a major source of entertainment for several millennia. In a famous passage from his 1757 work, *A Philosophical Enquiry into the Origin of Our Ideas of the Sublime and Beautiful,* the British philosopher Edmund Burke offered a striking hypothesis:

> Chuse a day on which to represent the most sublime and affecting tragedy we have; appoint the most favourite actors; spare no cost upon the scenes and decorations; unite the greatest efforts of poetry, painting and music; and when you have collected your audience, just at the moment when their minds are erect with expectation, let it be reported that a state criminal of high rank is on the point of being executed in the adjoining square; in a moment the emptiness of the theater would demonstrate the comparative weakness of the imitative arts, and proclaim the triumph of the real sympathy.[19]

Burke's point was that, if given the choice between witnessing an actual death and a dramatic representation, the audience would always opt for the former. By the late 1800s, however, audiences no longer had that choice. Watching a victim die agonizingly in public—broken on the wheel, burned alive, drawn and quartered, beheaded, or subjected to any one of scores of savage torments—had been outlawed by most civilized societies. From that point on, audiences would have to make do with dramatic imitation—with mere illusion.

By a happy coincidence, at that precise historical moment, the greatest illusion-making device ever contrived by human ingenuity had just been invented. It was called the motion picture camera—and from the very first, its unique ability to conjure realistic images of shocking, violent death accounted, in large measure, for its explosive success.

Torture for Dummies

•

Alook at the history of violent entertainment makes it very clear that—as the ethical values of Western society evolved over the centuries—simulated horrors were substituted for the actual atrocities which, in earlier ages, were performed on flesh-and-blood beings. Certainly, this is the case with torture. Long after this barbaric practice was abolished in the West, people continued to be fascinated by it. To cash in on this morbid interest, enterprising exhibitors mounted displays of old-fashioned torture devices, complete with lifelike dummies arranged in suitably agonized poses. The best-known of these was the "Chamber of Horrors" at Madame Tussaud's world-famous museum, where visitors could thrill to grisly tableaux featuring replicas of medieval torture implements along with realistic wax effigies of suffering victims.

In succeeding decades, technological advances made it possible to create ever more vivid displays of this sort, in which the various components of the diorama—from the hooded torturer to the writhing

(continued)

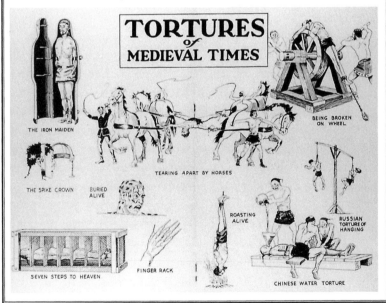

TORTURES *of* MEDIEVAL TIMES

THE IRON MAIDEN

BEING BROKEN ON WHEEL

THE SPIKE CROWN

BURIED ALIVE

TEARING APART BY HORSES

ROASTING ALIVE

RUSSIAN TORTURE OF HANGING

SEVEN STEPS TO HEAVEN

FINGER RACK

CHINESE WATER TORTURE

victim—actually moved. One of the most remarkable examples appeared in (of all places) the 1933 Chicago World's Fair.

The theme of the fair—which occupied 424 acres on the shore of Lake Michigan and ran from May 27 to November 1—was "A Century of Progress." Intended as a gala celebration of the country's enormous strides in industry and science, the exposition featured hundreds of exhibits dedicated to everything from air travel and atomic energy to meat packing and aluminum lawn furniture. Fairgoers could enjoy a visit to the Kraft Mayonnaise Kitchen (where its "new food triumph," Miracle Whip, was first introduced to the world); marvel at a fully functioning, animatronic Holstein cow at the agricultural pavilion; and have their feet checked out by expert podiatrists at the Dr. Scholl's exhibit in the Hall of Science.

Far surpassing these attractions in popularity, however, was the Torture Chamber. Built by the New York City firm of Messmore and Damon, this exhibit consisted of a series of elaborately constructed dioramas depicting a variety of infamous devices: the wheel, the rack, the Iron Maiden, and so

(continued)

on. A souvenir booklet offered instructive lessons on historical methods of torture. In keeping with the overall theme of the fair, the introduction to this pamphlet touted the exhibit as a modern marvel of mechanical engineering:

The Torture Chamber . . . stands as one of the most unique exhibits of the Century of Progress. The figures are all life size and are filled with gears, cams, and levers, operated by electrical motors, and yet so well has the task been performed that in reality they seem to breathe, move, and actually live as they did hundreds of years ago.

The costuming and details are worked out with the greatest accuracy and all the tortures shown are exact copies of the fiendish forms used in the Middle Ages. In some cases the actual implements that were used are shown. So lifelike are the figures and so exact in reproduction that many people have been forced to turn away in horror, unwilling to witness "man's inhumanity to man." The effect is heightened by the close synchronization of sound to motion, made possible by the latest developments in the

(continued)

sound engineer's art. Thus in the Torture Chamber you not only see the tortures as they were practised in the Middle Ages, but you hear again the questioning of the inquisitor, as well as the screams and groans of the unfortunate victims.

The Torture Chamber was located in an area of the Fair that also included a freak show and a Midget Village (where, according to the official guidebook, "sixty Lilliputians live in their tiny houses, serve you with food, and entertain you with theatrical performances"). Needless to say, none of those attractions would be regarded as socially acceptable to-day—a fact which suggests that, for all the hand wringing over the debased state of contemporary American culture, it is less crude, in many ways, than it used to be.

Still, even more than Miracle Whip, the 1933 World's Fair Torture Chamber really was a sign of our progress as a civilization, since it showed that, in the span of only a few centuries—the blink of an eye in evolutionary terms—the citizens of Western society had renounced real torture as a form of entertainment and accepted counterfeit cruelty in its place: mechanical tricks performed with gears, cams, and levers and perpetrated on motorized dummies.

SEVEN

•

Increasingly in the last century, sadism has been supplied to the American public in massive doses in all its popular arts until, now, one out of every three trees cut down in Canada for paper-pulp has murder written on it when the presses roll.

—G. LEGMAN, *Love & Death (1949)*

No sooner had the motion picture camera been invented than pioneering filmmakers figured out a way to make it perform shockingly violent optical tricks. It's a striking fact that the very first special effect ever created for the movies was a graphic beheading. This cinematic landmark occurs in Thomas Edison's 1895 Kinetoscope short, *The Execution of Mary, Queen of Scots,* which—true to its title—consists of nothing more than a thirty-second scene of the title character stepping onto the scaffold, kneeling at the block, and having her head whacked off.

This grisly sequence was accomplished with the earliest known use of stop-motion photography. After the elaborately costumed Queen Mary (actually one of Edison's male employees, Robert Thomae) laid her head on the block, the camera was stopped, a dummy substituted for the actor, and the filming resumed, creating the illusion of single continuous take. For all its historical pretension, the short is little more than a mini-splatter movie, designed to provide morbid titillation under the usual guise of cultural edification.

Other cinematic pioneers were quick to perceive—and exploit—this particular feature of the motion picture camera: i.e., its unique ability to produce startlingly lifelike images of people being chopped to pieces. Sigmund Lubin, for example—a major figure in the nascent

motion picture industry—took the same shameless tack as Edison, of-fering grisly sensationalism under a high-minded pretext. During the Boxer Rebellion, Lubin turned out various phony newsreels of Chi-nese atrocities, which he peddled as bona fide war footage. In his 1900 short, *Chinese Massacring Christians,* for example, a group of costumed actors slice off the head of a missionary, then gloat over the mutilated corpse; while *Beheading of a Chinese Prisoner* (also 1900) is nothing more than Edison's *Execution of Mary, Queen of Scots* in Asiatic garb

Georges Méliès—the French magician-turned-filmmaker, often regarded as the "Father of Special Effects"—likewise reveled in simu-lated decapitations. Besides such comical "tricks films" as *The Melo-maniac* (1903) and *The Terrible Turkish Executioner* (1904)—both of which feature multiple beheadings—Méliès, like Edison, produced costumed recreations like *Les derniers moments d'Anne de Boleyn* (1905) that allowed the audience to enjoy guilt-free gore by presenting it as weighty historical drama.

These and other graphic depictions of summary execution and capital punishment (Edison's *Shooting Captured Insurgents,* Lubin's *Exe-cution of a Spanish Spy,* Méliès' *Massacre en Crête*) illustrate a point made by Erwin Panofsy in his celebrated 1934 essay, "Style and Medium in the Motion Pictures": that, to evolve from a mere optical novelty into a medium of mass entertainment, motion pictures had to satisfy the audience's taste not only for sentimentality, slapstick, and sex, but also, very importantly, for sadistic spectacle. [1] Another film historian, Philip French, offers a similar argument in his widely reprinted essay, "Violence in the Cinema." "There never has been a time when the movies have not been preoccupied with violence," French points out, referring to Edison's *Execution of Mary, Queen of Scots,* as well as to the popular prizefight newsreels that American filmmakers began churning out as soon as movies were invented. Indeed, he insists, there is something in the very nature of the medium that makes it "tend towards violence": "The movies are predominantly about things happening, and the extreme form of things happening is violence. As everyone knows, the final word before shooting a scene is the director's call for 'Action.' Not surprisingly, to the moviemaker and the moviegoers the words 'action' and 'violence' as relating to the content of a film are virtually synonymous."

Because of "this natural violent bent," French argues, the movies have long since become our culture's primary means for fulfilling the "legitimate and enduring need" of the popular audience for vicarious aggression.[2] French quotes a lyric sung by Sammy Davis, Jr. in the 1964 Rat Pack romp, *Robin and the Seven Hoods,* by way of summing up the cheerfully homicidal fantasies that motion pictures have now been serving up for more than a century:

> *I like the fun,*
> *Of reaching for a gun,*
> *And going, Bang! Bang!*

That the movies have always relied on graphic "gratuitous" violence to bring in the crowds is clear from Edwin Porter's *The Great Train Robbery* (1903), far and away the most popular film of the first decade of the American cinema. This landmark motion picture is revered by film scholars for Porter's pioneering camera work and editing—his clever cutting between scenes of simultaneous action, his use of "pans" to follow the movement within a scene. Certainly, these devices made the film a uniquely kinetic experience for turn-of-the-century moviegoers who were used to watching films shot from stationary viewpoints and assembled in a plodding, strictly linear way.

What really made *The Great Train Robbery* so revolutionary at the time of its release, however, was the sheer level of violence it contained. Apart from its technical innovations, Porter's twelve-minute film was the first movie to demonstrate the point so lyrically made by Sammy Davis, Jr.: "the fun of reaching for a gun and going, *Bang! Bang!*" The prototypical Western, the movie is pure shoot-'em-up action—*Butch Cassidy and the Sundance Kid* with all of the boring stuff eliminated (character development, exposition, dialogue, etc.).

The storyline, as Gerald Mast and Bruce Kawin sum it up, goes as follows: "The outlaws enter the telegraph office and tie up the operator, board the train as it stops for water, rob the mail car and shoot the railroad man, seize the locomotive, unhook it from the rest of the train, rob all the passengers and shoot one who tries to escape, run to the locomotive and chug off, get off the locomotive and run to their horses in the woods." The film then cuts back to the telegraph office, where the bound operator is discovered. Cut again to a barn dance, where the townsmen are alerted to the crime. Next, we cut to the chase. The posse goes after the outlaws, who are dispatched in a blaze of gunfire.[3]

The movie concludes with a shot that—insofar as it is completely extraneous, serving no function whatsoever other than to provide a violent thrill—is the very definition of "gratuitous." A mustachioed bandit filmed in close-up raises his six-shooter and fires it directly at the camera. Audiences—as intended—went wild. (Describing the effect of this footage on contemporary filmgoers, the 1904 Edison catalogue declared "the resulting excitement is great.") The message conveyed by this (very literal) shot couldn't have been clearer: a new medium had arrived with the power to blow away viewers with its graphic, in-your-face depictions of violence.

To modern eyes, of course, the gunplay in *The Great Train Robbery* seems touchingly innocent, the quaint relic of a time when a bullet from a bad guy's pistol would cause a dying victim to fling his arms skyward and perform triple pirouettes before collapsing to the ground. To Porter's contemporaries, however, the onscreen violence was as thrillingly real as a computerized "shooter" game is to today's adolescents.

Of course, there are plenty of people around who will dispute this claim. Tell most senior citizens that the pop culture of their child-hoods was every bit as "bad"—i.e., as titillatingly violent—as today's and you'll get an indignant, "Nonsense! You can't compare the two!" And in one respect, they'd be right. In terms of frenetic pacing, py-rotechnical destruction, and sheer body count, there is in fact no com-parison between, say, a *Die Hard* movie and John Ford's *Stagecoach*. The *effect* of the two films on their respective audiences, however, was much the same. For little boys in 1939, *Stagecoach* was *Die Hard*—a fast-paced action movie that set their hearts racing, filled their heads with violent daydreams, and inspired them to play at make-believe mayhem. If anything, the impact of *Stagecoach* may have been even greater, since its original audience had never seen anything so exciting.

There is ample documentation of the overwhelming effect that early movies had on their viewers. When the Lumière brothers first screened *L'Arriveé de'un train en gare*—an 1895 short showing a loco-motive pulling into a railway station—the Parisian audience reputedly "shrieked and ducked when it saw the train hurtling toward them."[4] Thirty years later—to cite another famous example—Sir Arthur Co-nan Doyle, who was engaged in a feud with his former friend, Harry Houdini, showed up at a meeting of the Society of American Magi-cians with a test reel from the movie, *The Lost World,* depicting two puppet-animated dinosaurs fighting to the death. To our eyes, this se-quence (the handiwork of Willis O'Brien, the special-effects genius behind the original *King Kong*) seems about as realistic as an outtake from *Gumby.* Doyle's audience, however—which included Adolph S. Ochs, publisher of *The New York Times*—was so astonished by the scene that, the following day, the *Times* ran a front-page story proclaiming that Sherlock Holmes's creator had somehow managed to get hold of footage of living prehistoric beasts.

Examples could be multiplied ad infinitum. Todd Browning's *Dracula*—a film that strikes a modern viewer as high camp—caused 1931 moviegoers to swoon in their seats. "I saw the first fifteen minutes and could stand no more," attested Marjorie Ross Davis, a PTA executive who demanded that the film "be withdrawn from public viewing" because its "insane horrible details" were certain to "do an infinite amount of harm" to "children and the weak-minded."[5] When Jack Palance gunned down Elisha Cook, Jr., in *Shane,* causing the victim to go flying backwards into the mud from the force of the blast, the effect on 1953 viewers was shattering; no one had ever witnessed such brutally realistic screen violence before (prior to that time, people shot at close range tended to clutch their bellies and pitch forward).

The claim put forth by countless alarmists—that everything from the Columbine massacre to the "Beltway Sniper" shootings can be blamed on violent movies and video games—is largely based on the premise that today's technologically sophisticated pop fantasies are particularly pernicious because they seem so real. But the state-of-the-art pop entertainments of past eras were no less real or stimulating to their audiences (think, for example, of the mass hysteria provoked by Orson Welles's infamous 1938 radio production of *The War of the Worlds,* a broadcast that seems hopelessly hokey to a modern listener). Popular works that seem utterly innocuous to us—the product of more innocent times—were, in their own day, condemned for precisely the same reason that today's mass media scapegoats are: for creating illusions of violence so intense and convincing that impressionable young minds were bound to be corrupted by them.

Certainly this was the case with *The Great Train Robbery.* In 1912— as Kevin Brownlow points out in his indispensable study, *Behind the*

Mask of Innocence—the following page-one headline appeared in the Philadelphia *Record*:

BOY IS TO HANG FOR PICTURE PLAY

•

**Young Bishie's Express Robbery Tragedy
an Exact Reproduction from "Movies"
Slew Trusting Friend
Waited for Whistle at Long Curve So the Shot
Would Not be Heard**

According to the accompanying article, a young man named Fred Bishie had held up a train after seeing Porter's film in December 1911. Bishie had also slain an accomplice at the time of the crime, waiting until the whistle sounded before pulling the trigger. There were, as it happens, serious reasons to question the newspaper's claim. For one thing—though *The Great Train Robbery* was, in fact, playing at a theater in Scranton at the time of the incident—there was no indication that the accused had ever seen it. And even if he *had,* the movie couldn't possibly have suggested the train whistle ploy, since there is no such scene in Porter's film.

Still, the mere fact that a deadly train robbery occurred while Porter's film was showing in a nearby theater was all the proof that some people needed to pin Bishie's crime on the movies. By that time, as Brownlow points out—barely sixteen years after they were invented—motion pictures already had a history of being blamed for all sorts of social ills. Brownlow quotes one child-rearing expert of that era who—when asked "what proportion of disciplinary cases were attributable to movies"—replied without hesitation: "I should say they almost all were."[6]

In 1911, of course, the movies were just the latest in a long line of popular media to incur the outrage of moralists. What's so interesting about the antipop campaigns that have now been going on for several hundred years is how exactly alike they are. The pattern is always the same. A new medium of mass entertainment comes along that is aimed at—or embraced primarily by—kids and the working class. Very quickly, high-minded reformers begin to denounce it as a sign of social decay, a corrupter of the young, a threat to the very existence of civilization as we know it.

Sometimes, these crusades coincide with a surge in the crime rate, though just as often (as is the case today) they occur during a statistical dip. No matter. Examples are adduced that purportedly demonstrate a direct correlation between the commission of sensational crimes and the consumption of the latest form of violent make-believe. Eventually, with the advent of a new technology, another, more exciting, fast-paced, and action-packed pastime is created and the onetime media menace comes to be looked at nostalgically as a harmless, old-fashioned form of play. In retrospect, moreover, it is clear that—for all the hysteria of the moment—none of the dire predictions came true. The little readers of dime novels didn't turn into a generation of outlaws. The boys who thrilled to *Little Caesar* and *Public Enemy* didn't grow up to be tommy gun–toting gangsters. The teenage fans of *Halloween* and *Friday the 13th* didn't put on hockey masks and run out to dismember coeds with chainsaws.

During the heyday of the penny dreadful, for example, those cheap, sensationalistic publications were directly blamed for virtually every incident of juvenile crime in England. "There isn't a boy or a young lad tried at our Courts of Justice," proclaimed Sir Thomas Chambers, recorder of the City of London, "whose position there is not more or less due the effect of unwholesome literature upon his mind."[7] A half century later, however, old men who, in their youth, had devoured every installment of *The Wild Boys of London* and *Nick Carter, Detective* were waxing sentimental over those simple faraway pleasures. In 1948, for example, a venerable British gent, Capt. C. B. Fry, wrote an impassioned defense of the penny dreadfuls, arguing that they were "ten times" less harmful than the pop diversions of the modern era. Fry's most caustic words were reserved for two forms of commercial entertainment in particular: "the baser sort of cinema" and the "moronic" lyrics sung by radio crooners. While it's hard to conceive of Rudy Vallee and der Bingle as representing a serious threat to civilization, Captain Fry felt otherwise, insisting that "cretinous croon-words," along with "silly cinema," were a "modern fungus" on society. Not only did they "vitiate the general taste"; their artificial depictions of life made both "youth and maiden functionally unable to face things as they are."[8]

In the age of Eminem, it's funny to hear Fry working himself into a lather over "Life is Just a Bowl of Cherries" and "I'm Just a Vagabond Lover." But the old captain's diatribe illustrates a serious and highly pertinent point: namely that, for centuries, every time a new form of pop entertainment has appeared on the scene and been embraced by the young, their elders have gone into a panic over it.

In precartoon days, English children got their share of knockabout fun from watching Punch and Judy. That wildly popular show inspired the same sort of outrage that, in our own time, has been provoked by *Beavis and Butt-Head* and *South Park*. Denouncing its gleeful celebration of vice and utter contempt for "law and order," a Victorian critic named Hoffman could only explain the popularity of "The Punch and Judy Show" by seeing it as a "curious illustration of the depravity of human nature."[9] And in exactly the same way that today's moral guardians claim that watching violent images on TV makes kids more aggressive, the novelist George Meredith argued that "the puppet-show of 'Punch and Judy' inspires our street-urchins to have instant recourse to their fists in a dispute, after the fashion of every one of the actors in that public entertainment who gets possession of the cudgel."[10]

It is not without irony that the art form practiced by Meredith himself began life as a target of moralistic outrage. The first truly pop medium of the modern world, the novel, came under attack from the moment of its invention. In 1741, just a year after the publication of Samuel Richardson's *Pamela* (widely regarded by literary historians as the first modern novel), tracts were circulating in London condemning the book for its corrupting effects on "youth of both sexes."

Richardson's sentimental story of a poor but virtuous servant girl who must fight to maintain her chastity under the assaults of a vile seducer, was, according to its critics, certain to fill the minds of innocent readers with "lewd ideas" and inflame them with "emotions far distant from the Principles of Virtue."[11]

Nowadays—when parents struggle to get their kids to turn off the TV or PlayStation and read an occasional book—it's hard to conceive of a time when literature was regarded as a threat to the mental and moral well-being of the young. But for the first hundred-plus years of its existence, the novel provoked precisely the same kind of hysterical denunciations that have since been leveled at every new form of mass entertainment. "The evil consequences attendant upon novel reading are much greater than has generally been imagined," thundered Yale professor Samuel P. Jarvis during a speech in 1806. Popular fiction was decried as a contaminant that served "to enervate the youthful mind," "pollute the imaginations of young women," and transform its susceptible readers into "the slaves of vice."[12] Thomas Jefferson himself, that epitome of the Enlightenment, had this to say of the novel: "When this poison infects the mind, it destroys its tone and revolts it against wholesome reading. . . . The result is a bloated imagination, sickly judgment, and disgust towards all the real business of life."[13]

By the early nineteenth century, self-proclaimed experts on child rearing were issuing the same sort of parental warnings that their modernday counterparts offer in relation to television shows and Internet Web sites. "Parents, know what books your children read," advises the anonymous author of an 1820 screed published by the American Tract Society. "Leave not such a matter to chance, to giddiness, or vice. A bad book is poison. If you love misery, give novels to your children."[14]

Another pamphlet issued by this same organization distinguishes between good books ("works of science, art, history, theology, etc.") and bad ("books of fiction, romance, infidelity, war, piracy and murder"). The latter "insult the understanding of the reader by assuming that the great object of reading is amusement":

Beware of bad books because *they waste your time.* "Time is money"; it is more—it is *eternity!* You live in a sober, redeemed world, and it is worse than folly to fritter away the period of probation in mere amusement. . . . Beware of bad books because principles imbibed and images gathered from them *will abide in the memory and imagination for ever.* The mind once polluted is never freed from its corruption—never, unless by an act of boundless grace, through the power of the spirit of God.

Not content with condemning "books of mere fancy and fiction" as "corrupters of the community," the author of this tract flatly declares that fiction writers "are commonly bad men" whose "wicked character" is reflected in the unwholesome content of their books. Particularly to be avoided was the "foul and exciting romance," a "class of fiction" that "chooses scenes from the places of debauchery and crime, and familiarizes the reader with characters, sentiments, and events that should be introduced only to the police. Licentious scenes and obscene imagery are unblushingly introduced, and the imagination polluted by suggestions and descriptions revolting to the pure at heart." Such books—along with equally insidious novels about "war, piracy, and murder"—"stimulate the love of adventurous daring, cultivate the baser passions, and prompt to deeds of infamy. Away with them!" At the end of this diatribe, the writer exhorts his audience to take a solemn pledge: "*Henceforth, I will beware of bad books, and never read what can intoxicate, pollute, or deprave the mind and heart.*"[15]

Reading this diatribe, it's easy to assume that the writer must be talking about works of quasi-pornographic Victorian-era sensationalism, though the only author he denounces by name is Sir Walter Scott. But of course, the American Tract Society was a Christian organization whose puritanical assaults on all the evils of "trifling amusement" are echoed today in the hysterics of Bible Belt crusaders who see the hand of Satan in everything from Harry Potter to Scooby-Doo.

The enemies of nineteenth-century popular fiction, however, were not all fundamentalists. Brander Matthews, for example—Columbia professor and one of the most eminent literary figures of his day—denounced the dime novel in the most vehement terms. "The dreadful damage wrought today in every city, town, and village of these United States by the horrible and hideous stuff set weekly before the boys and girls of America by the villainous sheets which pander greedily and viciously to the natural taste of young readers for excitement—the irreparable wrong done by these vile publications—is hidden from no one," he railed in 1883.[16] Matthews's sentiments were echoed by countless educators and moral reformers who blamed the dime novel for everything from truancy to serial murder. In post–Civil War Boston, for example, critics did not hesitate to attribute the crimes of Jesse Harding Pomeroy—an adolescent psychopath who committed a string of atrocities that began with assault and escalated into mutilation-murder—to his supposed addiction to such insidious fare as *Bullethead Bill, the Colorado Bravo* and *Fred Fearnot's Close Call, or, Raiders of the Rawhide Range.*[17]

It wasn't until forty years after his famous attack on "cheap blood-and-thunder fiction" that Professor Matthews himself publicly confessed that, during his own boyhood, he had been an ardent fan of "the saffron-backed Dime Novels of the late Mr. Beadle." Reminiscing about these disreputable diversions from the

380 "Biz," sternly said the anti-tobacco crusader, "even a hog will not chew that vile weed!" "Aw, well, replied poor old Dodd Durnit. "I never keered especially about having a hog regulate my diet, no-way."

vantage point of old age, he now praised them for their "ultra-Puritan purity" and "their thrilling and innocuous record of innocent and imminent danger."[18] By then, of course, the dime novel had long been supplanted by new and presumably more pernicious forms of pop entertainment that made Mr. Beadle's once-demonized offerings seem positively wholesome.

One of these was the comic strip. Hard as it is to believe about the genre that produced *Krazy Kat, Li'l Abner,* and *Pogo,* the newspaper "funnies" were once widely condemned not just as lowbrow trash but as a leading cause of mental and moral degeneracy among the young. As early as 1907, a magazine called the *Independent* sounded the alarm about the comic section of the Sunday paper—the "vicious colored supplement" that "cannot help but vitiate taste and deprave intelligence." By 1909, with the anticomic-strip crusade in full swing, *The Ladies Home Journal* described the Sunday funnies as "A Crime Against the Children of America" and denounced as "criminally negligent" any parent who allowed such insidious fare as *Mutt & Jeff* and *The Katzenjammer Kids* into the home. Not to be outdone, the *Journal*'s main competitor—*Good Housekeeping*—railed against the Sunday funnies as "a carpet of hideous caricatures, crude art, and poverty of invention, perverted humor, obvious vulgarity, and rudest coloring . . . which makes for lawlessness, debauched fancy, irreverence."[19]

Needless to say, these and similar diatribes did not make a dent in the popularity of the funnies which, of course, were eagerly gobbled up every weekend by young and old alike. Indeed, by the 1930s the genre had expanded to include a whole new kind of strip for which the term "funnies" was a serious misnomer, since it wasn't meant to elicit yuks like earlier "gag" comics. Full of two-fisted action and high-spirited melodrama, these graphic adventure serials—*Flash Gordon, Dick Tracy, Secret Agent X-9,* etc.—sent moralists into even greater frenzies of disapproval, best epitomized, perhaps, by a rabid assault published in a 1936 issue of *The Forum* by a critic named John K. Ryan.

Ryan's lead is certainly a grabber—a catalogue of the "debased and debasing features of the comic strips" that sounds like one of the rants that used to be delivered on *Saturday Night Live* by Dana Carvey's Church Lady:

> Sadism, cannibalism, bestiality. Crude eroticism. Torturing, killing, kidnapping. Monsters, madmen, creatures half-brute, half-human. Raw melodrama; tales of crimes and criminals; extravagant exploits in strange lands and on other planets; pirate stories; wild, hair-raising adventures of boy heroes and girl heroines; thrilling accounts in words and pictures of jungle beasts and men; marvelous deeds of magic and pseudoscience. Vulgarity, cheap humor, and cheaper wit. Sentimental stories designed for the general level of the moronic mind. Ugliness of thought and expression. All these, day after day, week after week, have become the mental food of American children, young and old. With such things are the comic strips that take up page upon page in the average American newspaper filled.

In answer to his own rhetorical question—"Is a continuous diet of lurid melodrama, told by pictures of brutal men doing brutal deeds, good for children?"—Ryan proceeds to cite specific examples of the daily horrors dished out in the comics to "mentally immature" youngsters and "emotionally unstable" adults. An installment of *Dick Tracy* in which the "repulsive hunchbacked villain" is set upon by a vicious dog that "is shown tearing at the hunchback's throat while Junior and Tracy look on in horror." An episode of *Flash Gordon* in which the hero, captured by "horrible lizard men," is "ordered thrown upon a flaming griddle to be cooked for their cannibalistic feast." A *Tarzan* strip in which two American starlets are abducted by mutant talking apes and subjected to a "hideous" ordeal of "bestiality and sadism." A sequence from *Jungle Jim* in which the Chinese bad guy, Cho Fang, "has captured Jim's friend, Fah See, also Chinese, and is torturing him. Naked, except for the irreducible minimum of the loincloth, Fah See is being stretched upon the rack. When he refuses to give information, he is tortured until he faints. Cho Fang then orders that he be thrown into the pit, where the rats will finish him off."[20]

That Ryan's tirade against *Jungle Jim* and *Dick Tracy* (like Brander Matthews's denunciation of Deadwood Dick, George Meredith's attack on "Punch and Judy," Captain Fry's condemnation of radio crooners, etc., etc.) seems so comically overwrought to us should serve as a warning to contemporary crusaders who wax equally hysterical over today's popular culture, and whose fulminations are likely to seem just as excessive in the future, when early 21st-century pop diversions like "Grand Theft Auto" and *Jackass: The Movie* are looked back upon as hopelessly quaint.

Menace to Their Ears

•

Created by an artist with an unreserved scorn for the vulgarity of contemporary popular culture, Woody Allen's 1978 film *Radio Days* conveys a powerful longing for the innocent diversions of his 1940s boyhood, when the airwaves were filled—not with the barbaric yawp of rock 'n' roll (let alone rap) or the Philistine fare of network TV—but with the presumably more wholesome and sophisticated pleasures of *Inner Sanctum, Lux Radio Theater,* and *Fibber McGee and Molly.* What Allen's cinematic paean leaves out of the picture, however, is the extent to which radio itself—like every other form of mass entertainment invented since the 1700s—was savaged in its heyday by censorious critics, who condemned it as a corrupt commercial medium responsible for degrading the minds and morals of the great American public.

Almost from the instant of its invention, radio came under fire for betraying its cultural potential. As early as 1927, critics were complaining that—instead of improving listeners by exposing them to the uplifting strains of operas,

(continued)

classical music, and the like— broadcasters were pandering to the lowest common denominator by filling the airwaves with "the rattle and bang of incredibly frightful 'jazz' music." A quarter century later, Lee deForest—one of the pioneers of the medium and the self-described "Father of Radio"—was still lamenting the uses to which his "child" had been put by network executives who cared about nothing except selling airtime to advertisers:

What have you gentlemen done with my child? He was conceived as a potent instrumentality for culture, fine music, the uplifting of America's mass intelligence. You have debased this child, you have sent him out in the streets in rags of ragtime, tatters of jive and boogie woogie, to collect money from all and sundry, for hubba bubba and audio jitterbug. You have made him a laughingstock to the intelligence, surely a stench to the gods of the ionosphere.

DeForest went even further. Children, he claimed, were being "rendered psychopathic" by the swill coming over the airwaves. The culprit here was not the hideous "hubba bubba" of ragtime, jive, and boogie-woogie but—predictably enough—the "blood-and-thunder" radio melodramas that had supplanted dime novels and gangster movies as the favorite whipping boy of tongue-clucking moralists.

The assault on radio violence began in earnest in the 1930s, when popular magazines were filled with articles like "Radio Horror: For Children Only," "Radio Gore Criticized," and "The Children's Hour of Crime." Writing in the May 1933 issue of *Scribner's* magazine, for example, a critic named Arthur Mann accused such popular programs as *Little Orphan Annie, Buck Rogers,* and *Bobby Benson of the H-Bar-O Ranch* of glorifying "every form of crime known to man," from kidnapping and extortion to assault and "sadistic abuse." Mann recommended that parents follow his example by removing the power tube from their Zeniths and Philcos between the hours of four and eight P.M. each day—the prime radio time for juvenile listeners. This early version of today's V-chip technology would protect impressionable youngsters from "four hours of

(continued)

lessons on the art of crime and higher skullduggery."

The noxious effect that action-adventure radio serials presumably had on their kiddie listeners was vividly described in a 1937 article in *Newsweek*:

They shudder delightedly while guns belch yellow flame and heads are split and hearts are broken. They gasp as airplanes roar down through imaginary skies to drop bombs. And their eyes widen appreciatively when men die suddenly on city pavements or wield blunt instruments with deplorable results.

In a tradition that goes back to the early nineteenth century—when penny dreadfuls were blamed for turning young readers into highwaymen—radio melodramas were accused of inciting criminal behavior in their juvenile audiences, a charge typified by the statements of the New York City Police commissioner who claimed that the perpetrators of a sensational kidnapping in Depression-era Manhattan had gotten the idea directly from a popular radio show called *Eno Crime Clues*.

Needless to say, the same sorts of accusations are still being leveled today, though now the prime targets are violent movies, TV shows, and video games. In the wake of the Columbine massacre, for example, pundits were quick to point out that the juvenile perpetrators had been fascinated by the violent sci-fi thriller, *The Matrix*. A grisly dismemberment that occurred in early 2003 was immediately connected to a parallel scene in an episode of *The Sopranos*. And at the height of the so-called Beltway Sniper crime spree, various experts appeared on TV to announce that the killer had undoubtedly honed his skills by playing video "shooter" games.

According to today's antipop crusaders, what makes movies, television shows, and video games far more dangerous than the commercial entertainments of the past is their kinetic, visual imagery, which presumably exerts an irresistible power over the minds of viewers, especially young ones. Significantly however, the exact opposite argument was advanced in the 1930s. Back then, critics insisted that radio had a uniquely harmful impact on children precisely because it was *not* a visual medium but rather an aural one. The sound of a murder victim's skull being smashed, or of a

(continued)

convict being executed in the electric chair (actions simulated in the studio by, respectively, breaking open a cantaloupe and frying some bacon) was far worse, it was claimed, than the sight of such violence. In an 1932 article in the *Journal of Adult Education*. for example, a writer named Lyman Bryson argued that the eye—being a more sensitive and discriminating organ than the ear—was better able to distinguish make-believe from reality. People, especially children, were especially vulnerable to the violence transmitted over the radio, since it affected them on the more "primitive," less critically sophisticated level of hearing. [21] Or as film critic Roger Ebert put it in recalling the "physical intensity" of his response to the radio programs of his youth, the TV shows and movies he watched as a child happened on screen, but radio "happened in my head."

That today's antipop crusaders denounce movie and video violence because it is visual—while their counterparts in the 1930s attacked radio crime shows because they were transmitted aurally—and Victorian reformers deplored the dime novel because it was written in a sensational, subliterate style—leads one to conclude that it doesn't really matter *what* the medium is. The real issue is that there will always be people who are incensed by violent entertainment, whether it is transmitted via sound or image, print or pixel; and that the current uproar over popular culture is simply part of a never-ending cycle of outrage that will undoubtedly go on into the future, when today's controversial cinematic and video shoot-'em-ups will come to seem as harmless as the average episode of *The Shadow* or *Captain Midnight*.

Ryan, of course, was not the only critic to get worked up over kiddie amusements that, from our own perspective, seem almost touching in their charm, innocence, and craftsmanship. In 1947, for example, John Houseman—known to a later generation as the spokesman for the Smith Barney brokerage firm ("We make money the old-fashioned way") but famed in his younger years as Orson Welles's collaborator and a prize-winning producer, director, and actor on his own—published an article in *Vogue* on Hollywood's then-current infatuation with "tough-guy" pictures like *The Big Sleep* and *The Post-man Always Rings Twice.* Before getting to his main subject, Houseman had some things to say about the level of violence in American popular culture in general. Like John K. Ryan ten years earlier, he was harshly critical of newspaper comic strips that were "devoted, with few exceptions, to incidents of lawless brutality. A random perusal of the comic sections of last Sunday's metropolitan papers yielded a harvest of no less than seven murders (the lifeless bodies of the victims being exhibited in four instances), two robberies with violence, one case of torture, two cases of criminal assault, and one of abduction with clear intent to rape—not to mention numerous instances of hillbilly mayhem and inter-planetary violence."[22]

Even worse in Houseman's view was a genre closely related to the newspaper "funnies"—i.e., the animated cartoon that constituted such a vital part of the matinee moviegoing experience for American youngsters. "I remember the time," he wistfully writes,

> when Disney and his less successful imitators concerned themselves with the frolicsome habits of bees, birds, and the minor furry animals. *Joie-de-vivre* was the keynote. . . . Now all this is changed. The fantasies which our children greet with howls of joy run red with horrible savagery. Today the animated cartoon has become a bloody battlefield through which savage and remorseless creatures, with single-track minds, pursue one another, then rend, gouge, twist, tear, and mutilate each other with sadistic ferocity.[23]

To read this passage, you'd think that Houseman was describing the extravagantly gruesome goings-on of Bart Simpson's favorite cartoon, *Itchy & Scratchy,* when, in fact, he's referring to what are now universally regarded as classics of the genre, the products of a Golden Age of Hollywood animation: Max Fleischer's *Popeye,* Walter Lantz's *Woody Woodpecker,* MGM's *Tom & Jerry,* Warner Brothers' *Looney Tunes* and *Merrie Melodies,* and so on.

The fact that—in 1947—a man of Houseman's intellectual sophistication could yearn for the supposedly more wholesome entertainments of the 1920s (when Disney and his peers turned out their earliest cartoons about the "frolicsome habits" of "minor furry animals"), while—in 2003—critics yearn for the presumably more innocent amusements of the 1940s and 1950s suggests that the perennial crusades against popular culture are, as much as anything else, an expression of nostalgia for an imaginary past that always seems simpler and more "childlike" than the harsh and complex reality of the here-and-now.

Certainly the pop culture of post–World War II America was experienced by many intellectuals of the time as deplorably crude and immoral. And among its critics, none was more unstinting in his contempt than Gershon Legman.

In biographical entries, Legman is often described as an intellectual "maverick," though even that characterization fails to do justice to a man who, among his other highly colorful accomplishments, did bibliographical research for Alfred Kinsey; became an expert on Japanese paper folding and helped introduce the art of origami to the West; published a massive, two-volume psychoanalytic study of the dirty joke and compiled the world's largest collection of obscene limericks; invented (so he claimed) the vibrating dildo and coined (so he also claimed) the slogan, "Make Love, Not War"; was a regular contributor to *Playboy;* and served as editor of the pioneering, if short-lived, little magazine, *Neurotica,* which published the earliest work of Allan Ginsburg and other young literary renegades soon to be known as the Beats.

It was in the pages of *Neurotica,* in fact, that Legman launched his first assaults on American popular culture, later collected in his 1949 diatribe, *Love & Death: A Study in Censorship.* Like John Houseman—whom he cites approvingly (even while taking him to task for producing "murder movies" of his own, like the 1946 thriller, *The Blue Dahlia*)—Legman inveighed against the animated cartoon and its prime purveyor, Walt Disney, who, in his typically intemperate view, was guilty of nothing less than the commercially motivated corruption of minors:

In our culture, the perversion of children has become an industry. When Mr. Walt Disney, the dean of that industry, sits down with his artists to put a nursery story into animated pictures, color, and sound, what do they do to it to insure their investment of time and money? What did they do to *The Three Little Pigs,* their greatest triumph? They changed a story of diligence rewarded and laziness punished, into a Grand Guignol of wolf-tortured-by-pigs, complete with house-sized "Wolf Pacifier" beating the wolf over the head with six rolling-pins, kicking him in the rump with as many automatic boots, and reserving bombs and TNT beneath, and a potty-chair overhead to finish him off with.[24]

Legman, however, did not limit his denunciations to Disney cartoons but excoriated the entire range of American mass entertainment. Comic books (the biggest pop bugaboo of the Eisenhower era, at least until Elvis came along) were "without exception principally, if not wholly, devoted to violence"—an accusation he leveled against every class of comic, from the "floppity-rabbit" variety (in which "little anthropomorphic animals" spend all their time "gouging, twisting, tearing, and mutilating one another") to *Classics Illustrated* (in which "all the most violent children's books of the last two centuries are condensed into forty-eight-page pictures-sequences, omitting every literary element . . . and squeezing together every violent scene that can be found in the original").

The paperback murder mysteries flooding the market represented nothing less than a "broken dam of literary bloodlust." Pulp magazines—"the sole reading, with the newspaper, of tens of millions at the threshold of literacy"—existed in two forms: "half of them straight murder, the other half divided up into an 'action' group that is mostly murder, too."

On the radio, reporters were now doing "spot-news broadcasts from the foot of the electric chair," while comedians engaged in nothing but verbal "abuse and blatherskite." And in the few years of its existence, TV had already degenerated from the "fantasy bloodlust" of early melodramas and cowboy shows to real-life "holocausts of berserk bone-crushing" in the form of televised prizefights and pro wrestling matches. Even more repulsive, in Legman's view, were shows like *Queen for a Day*—"audience humiliation programs (under the guise of confessionals and giveaways), capitalizing on mayhem and sadomasochism in the nth degree, with the payoff to the victims in re-frigerators."[25]

What's fascinating about Legman's book is that—while there is nothing in it that wouldn't win a hearty endorsement from William Bennet or Tipper Gore—his argument is founded on principles dia-metrically opposed to those of current-day crusaders, who dream of restoring our "X-rated society" (in Ms. Gore's phrase) to the presum-ably "G-rated" values that prevailed before the advent of the decadent

1960s. Relying on a reductive Freudianism, Legman be-lieved that America's obses-sion with media violence was a direct consequence of

our lingering sexual Puritanism—that, as he put it, "the maniacal fixation on violence and death in all our mass-produced fantasies is a substitution for censored sexuality." To glorify the gunplay of Billy the Kid in Howard Hughes's *The Outlaw* was fine; but to show "the groove between the breasts of Miss Jane Russell" in the same motion picture was sternly forbidden. "Death yes, sex no," was our culture's unspoken, pathological motto—or as Legman also, and somewhat more pungently, put it: "No tits—blood."

The only solution to this problem, in his view, was sexual liberation. Breaking down the dam of Puritanical repression would unleash a tide of healthy eroticism that would wash our pop culture clean of its obsessive sadism. To that end, Legman devoted himself to the exploration and celebration of then-taboo subjects, publishing, among other books, a three-hundred-plus-page treatise called *Ora-Genitalism: Oral Techniques in Genital Excitation,* in the apparent belief that more fellatio and cunnilingus in the bedroom would reduce the number of murders in movies and on TV. Or, as he might have put it, "More blowjobs—less bloodshed."

Time, however, has proven Legman wrong. Forty years into the revolution in societal mores that he yearned for and indeed helped to inspire, American popular culture is saturated with sexual imagery to an extent that even the pioneering author of *Ora-Genitalism,* in his most wildly utopian fantasies, probably couldn't have envisioned. And yet at a time when every erotic barrier appears to have fallen—when female pop stars like Alanis Morissette perform hit songs about going down on their boyfriends and newsstand magazines run fashion ads featuring S&M bondage shots more explicit than anything to be found in the sleaziest 1950s porno mag—media violence has obviously not subsided. If Legman thought that televised fifties-era wrestling bouts between Gorgeous George and Man Mountain Dean were "holocausts of berserk bone-crushing," what would he make of the average WWF "Raw is War" hardcore match in which steroid-enhanced behemoths go at each other with everything from metal garbage cans to folding chairs? And if *Queen for a Day* was an "audience humiliation" program that capitalized "on mayhem and sadomasochism in the nth degree," a new measure of magnitude of would have to be invented to describe the level of humiliation, mayhem, and sadomasochism in any given episode of *The Jerry Springer Show.*

Legman's simplistic equation ("No tits—blood") notwithstanding, it would appear that the amount of violence in a work of popular art isn't a function of its erotic content. What is often referred to as the "healthy bawdry" of Shakespeare's plays did not, after all, keep him from tossing in a bunch of graphic gore to keep the groundlings happy. As the preceding survey has shown, explicit violence has always been an integral feature of popular culture, and to an extent that has always dismayed the refined sensibilities of certain people. It appears to me that there is only one conclusion to be drawn from this fact—namely, that one of the main functions of the popular arts is precisely to supply us with fantasies of violence, to allow us to vent—safely, in a controlled, socially acceptable, vicarious way—those "undying primal impulses which, however outmoded by civilization, need somehow to be expressed" (as Leslie Fielder puts it).[26]

Along these lines, a quote from the critic George Stade seems particularly apt: "People are fascinated by representations of murder because, in the first place, they want to kill someone and, in the second, they won't. Surely one function of narrative is to allow in the imagination what we forbid in the flesh."[27] Of course, there are those who would strenuously deny Stade's assertion—that they have murder in their hearts. Others—myself included—would argue that it is precisely this discomfort with one's darkest urges that accounts for the perennial hostility towards the popular arts. Many people are afraid of their own dreams. But the point made by critics like Fiedler and Stade is that, far from being "gratuitous" and harmful, make-believe violence is necessary and even healthy—good for our sanity as individuals and as a community.

In short—contrary to Legman's belief—fantasy violence isn't a substitute for sex. It is a substitute for actual violence.

Spillane's Bloody Hammer

•

Given that their sense of the 1950s comes primarily from sitcom reruns on the TVLand cable network, it's easy to see why today's adolescents tend to believe that the popular culture of that time was all *I Love Lucy* innocence and *Leave It to Beaver* blandness. What's a bit harder to grasp is how people who grew up in the post–World War II period—boomer-era types like Senator Joseph Lieberman and conservative critic William Bennett—share the same sugar-coated view of that decade, invoking it as a Golden Age when the popular arts were devoid of the kind of graphic, gratuitous violence that supposedly distinguishes today's mass entertainment.

There are two likely explanations for this state of affairs. Either those in the Lieberman-Bennett camp led remarkably sheltered lives as young people, or—more probably—they have succumbed to that sentimentalizing tendency, common to the middle-aged, which censors out the unsavory realities of the past. For the fact is that—contrary to popular belief—there

was a shockingly high level of sadistic violence and gore in some of the most popular commercial entertainments of the 1950s. Anyone who doubts this assertion has either forgotten, willfully excluded from memory—or is simply to young to know—the once widely reviled name of Mickey Spillane.

A one-time writer for comic books and the "bloody pulps," Spillane hit it big in 1948 when Signet released the paperback edition of his first novel, *I, the Jury*. Reportedly written in nine days (Spillane often claimed that he never spent more than two weeks on a novel), the book sold in the millions, transforming him into an instant celebrity. Over the next few years, he established himself as a bona fide phenomenon, the Stephen King/Tom Clancy/John Grisham of his day. By 1951 he had written the three best-selling mystery novels of all time (*I, the Jury, My Gun is Quick, Vengeance is Mine*). In 1952, his fourth novel, *Kiss Me Deadly,* sold a then-unheard-of seventy-five thousand hardcover copies and topped both *The New York Times* and *Herald Tribune* best-seller lists. In a list of the biggest-selling books published in

(continued)

America between 1895 and 1955, seven of the top fifteen were by Spillane. Sales for individual titles like *The Big Kill* and *The Girl Hunters* were surpassed only such megasellers as *Gone with the Wind* and *Peyton Place.*

The hero of Spillane's blockbusters is his two-fisted alter ego, Mike Hammer, a wildly (not to say psychotically) brutal private eye who makes his fictional predecessors like Dashiell Hammett's Sam Spade and Raymond Chandler's Philip Marlowe look (to use Marlowe's own ultimate put down) like pansies. As Spillane's titles make abundantly clear, Hammer plays the role of judge, jury, and executioner, meting out savage vigilante justice to any evildoer who, as he puts it, "needs knocking off bad." Undeterred by such trivial considerations as due process, a suspect's civil rights, or the U. S. Constitution, he proceeds to track down and brutalize his favorite targets—commies, crooked cops, mafiosi, and assorted femmes fatale—with such sadistic glee that, by comparison, Clint Eastwood's Dirty Harry seems like a card-carrying member of the ACLU. "I loved to shoot killers," he declares in *Vengeance in Mine.* "I couldn't think of any-

thing I'd rather do than shoot a killer and watch his blood trace a slimy path across the floor."

Though this statement stands as a fair distillation of Hammer's credo, it is not entirely accurate since—in addition to shooting killers (usually in the gut, though not infrequently in the "gaping hole" formed by their mouths as they let out a horrified scream)—he also thoroughly enjoys smashing in their teeth, shattering their bones, laying open their scalps with the butt of his gun, and administering countless other brutalities, all described by Spillane in the most sickeningly graphic terms. So rife with outrageous, over-the-top violence are his books that it's hard to single out one representative passage, though this sample from *The Big Kill* will serve as well as any to provide a sense of the gloatingly sadistic flavor of his prose:

The goddamn bastards played right into my hands. They thought they had me nice and cold and just as they were set to carve me into a raw mess of skin, I dragged out the .45 and let them look down the hole so they could see where sudden death came from.

(continued)

It was the only kind of talk they knew. The little guy stared too long. He should have been watching my face. I snapped the side of the rod across his jaw and laid the flesh open to the bone. He dropped the sap and staggered into the big boy with a scream starting to come up out of his throat only to get it cut off in the middle as I pounded his teeth back into his mouth with the end of the barrel. . . . The punk was vomiting on the floor, trying to claw his way under the sink. For laughs I gave him a taste of his own sap on the back of his hand and felt the bones go into splinters. He wasn't going to be using any tools for a long time.

Even the most vehement critics of contemporary popular culture would be hard-pressed to find anything in today's mainstream mass entertainment as alarming as the gore-drenched, gun-worshipping fantasies that Spillane and his publisher dished out for the delectation of millions of ordinary American readers in the supposedly halcyon days of the 1950s.

Critics of the time were, of course, suitably outraged, accusing Spillane not only of literary crimes (to Anthony Boucher of *The New York Times* his novels were the "ultimate degradation" of the Hammett–Chandler tradition) but also of undermining the moral foundations of American society. *Life* magazine dubbed him "Death's Fair-Haired Boy," while the *San Francisco Chronicle* declared that *I, the Jury* set forth "so vicious a glorification of force, cruelty, and extralegal methods that the novel might be made required reading in a Gestapo training school." Spillane was also attacked in the pages of *Harper's, New Republic,* and, famously, the *Saturday Review,* where critic Christopher LaFarge accused him of promoting the fascistic philosophy of McCarthyism. In a lighter vein, satirist Ira Wallach caught the insanely sadistic tenor of Spillane's work in a pitch-perfect 1952 parody, *Me, the Judge:*

Peter Rivet believed in justice. When the killer struck, Pete swore he'd shoot him down, right through the gut, with a slug as big as a 14-ounce sinker. Then, when the killer was lying there with a slug in his belly, Pete swore he'd kick in his teeth. Then he'd jump on his face. Then he'd get a hacksaw and saw the body into parts.

(continued)

Then he'd jump on the parts. Then he'd smash the teeth on the hacksaw. Then he'd work over that louse of a hardware dealer who sold him a hacksaw with smashed teeth.

Another popular satirist of the day, the poet Ogden Nash, was moved to suggest that the violence in Spillane's work was shocking enough to unbalance the Marquis de Sade:

> The Marquis de Sade
> Wasn't always mad.
> What addled his brain
> Was Mickey Spillane.

Spillane took all the criticism with a disarming, self-deprecating charm, insisting that, though his books might be garbage, they were at least "good garbage." He also suggested that he had loaded his books with sadism as a matter of commercial calculation. "There was a time when wild, gory scenes of violence were stock items in a story or script," he told an interviewer in 1961. "I certainly went all out myself when that was the trend." There is reason to question this claim, since—as many critics have noted—the brute force of the Mike Hammer books seems to spring from a genuine place in the author. But Spillane is right to point out that "wild, gory scenes of violence" were an integral part of American popular culture in the late 1940s and 1950s—as, indeed, they have always been in the long history of mass entertainment.

EIGHT

•

Let him not quit his belief that a popgun is a popgun,
though the ancient and honorable of the earth affirm it to be
the crack of doom.

—RALPH WALDO EMERSON

Born in Bavaria in 1895, Fredric Wertham was educated in London, Paris, and Vienna and received his M.D. from the University of Würzburg in 1921. After corresponding with Freud, he decided to make psychiatry his life's work. Emigrating to the United States in 1922, he joined the prestigious Phipps Psychiatric Clinic at Johns Hopkins University, where he wrote *The Brain as Organ,* a book that would become a standard text in the field of neuropathology. Active in the city's thriving intellectual life, he joined H. L. Mencken's Saturday Club and befriended renowned trial lawyer Clarence Darrow, who often referred African-American patients to Wertham, one of the few psychiatrists of the time who would treat them.

In 1932, Wertham moved to New York City to take up the post of senior psychiatrist at Bellevue Hospital. Twelve years into his tenure—with the support of such luminaries as Richard Wright, Ralph Ellison, and Paul Robeson—he founded the LaFargue Clinic in Harlem, which offered psychological counseling to the disadvantaged for the nominal fee of twenty-five cents per visit. An article he wrote for *The Journal of American Psychotherapy*—"Psychological Effects of School Segregation"—served as a key piece of evidence in the landmark 1954 Supreme Court case, *Brown vs. Board of Education,* that led to the end of racial segregation in U.S. public schools.

During this period, Wertham also served as a consultant to the New

York City courts, testifying as an expert witness in scores of cases and offering recommendations that led to significant improvements in the kind of psychiatric treatment inmates received throughout the prison system.

From any unbiased perspective, Wertham was an estimable man, enlightened in his politics, humane in his concerns—someone who devoted his long career to doing genuinely good work on behalf of society and his fellow human beings. It is one of those nasty little life ironies, therefore, that—insofar as he is remembered at all—he exists in the memories of millions of boomer-age Americans as a figure of pure evil.

What earned Wertham his undying notoriety was his best-selling, luridly titled, 1954 polemic, *Seduction of The Innocent,* one of the most influential books of the decade and the culmination of a campaign that he had embarked on six years earlier. Like Gershon Legman (and in stark contrast to most moral crusaders today), Wertham was decidedly liberal in his sexual attitudes, and in 1948 he was asked to appear as a defense witness in the obscenity trial of *Sunshine and Health,* one of those tacky masturbation magazines passing itself off as a wholesome celebration of the nudist lifestyle during the pre-*Playboy* era. On the stand, Wertham testified that the magazine was neither pornographic nor salacious. If the court wanted to see something *really* obscene, he declared, he would be happy to oblige. Then—displaying that flair for the dramatic that would make him one of the most effective public speakers of his day—he reached inside his pocket and pulled out a crime comic book, which—so he pointedly said—he had purchased at a newsstand right outside the courthouse.

His gesture, reported in the press, caught the attention of Norman Cousins, editor of the *Saturday Review,* who invited him to contribute a piece on the evils of comic books. When the article—published in late May 1949—was reprinted in the August *Reader's Digest,* the anti–comic book crusade was fully launched, with Wertham leading the charge.

Published at a time when, according to one contemporary poll, juvenile delinquency ranked higher on the list of public concerns than open-air atom bomb testing, *Seduction of the Innocent* became an immediate best-seller and was excerpted in both *Reader's Digest* and *Ladies' Home Journal,* guaranteeing its maximum impact on the American middle-class.[1] Wertham's argument—based on his own experiences treating young offenders in Harlem and Queens (and therefore largely anecdotal in nature)—was simplicity itself: juvenile delinquents tend to be avid readers of crime comics; ergo, crime comics are a prime cause of juvenile delinquency.

This kind of reductive (and utterly meaningless) correlation has been used by moral crusaders since at least the time of the Victorians, when sex manuals offered graphic proof of the perils of masturbation by running pictures of "feebleminded" youths who were given to "self-abuse" (and whose mental deficiencies could therefore be blamed on their supposedly debilitating habit). Correlations, after all, are not causes: besides reading crime and horror comics, a majority of the troubled youngsters studied by Wertham also undoubtedly chewed gum, smoked cigarettes, and combed their duck's-ass haircuts with Brylcreem. And there were other problems with Wertham's position, not the least of which was the fact that, despite the nationwide panic over the issue, juvenile crime in the early 1950s was *not* more common than it had been in the past. Indeed, according to one study, the arrest rate for young adolescents in New York City was five times *lower* in 1950 than it had been in 1907 (back then, of course, child-rearing mavens had their own explanation for the moral deterioration of America's youth: dime novels).[2]

Various specialists in the fields of psychology, sociology, and criminology took vehement exception to Wertham's claims, scoffing at his simplistic "monocausal" analysis. In the December 1949 issue of the *Journal of Educational Sociology,* for example—which was entirely devoted to the comic book controversy—juvenile delinquency expert Frederic Thrasher pointed out that "serious studies of mass culture have found no correlation at all between imaginary violence and the spread of youth crime," while reading expert Josette Frank and NYU professor Harvey Zorbaugh cited various studies that showed that reading comics offered significant emotional benefits to many under-age readers, "satisfying the perfectly normal needs of childhood."

The notion that comic books could actually be good for kids was corroborated by Katherine Wolfe and Marjorie Fiske of the Bureau of Applied Social Research at Columbia University, who insisted that the only children who might be harmed by comics were those who were maladjusted to begin with. The people most likely to be incited to violence by these unpretentious publications, Wolfe and Fiske noted dryly, were parents, whose whose anger "erupted in the form of hostile letters to the editor, blaming comics for everything from the children's bad language to international crises."[3]

Despite these voices of moderation, the parents of America—along with a legion of pundits and politicians—rallied around Wertham's cause. For unexplained reasons, the hysteria over juvenile delinquency was especially acute in the years between 1953 and 1956, and Wertham's book pinpointed a ready and superficially plausible villain— i.e., corrupt pop entertainment—one, moreover, that, in its various incarnations from Victorian penny dreadfuls to Depression-era pulp magazines, had a long and proven history of serving as a satisfactory scapegoat.

In the time-honored way of many high-minded exposés, Wertham's book also offered its proper middle-class audience a prime opportunity for guilt-free titillation, allowing them to slaver over its most juicy tidbits while simultaneously clucking their tongues. Like the infamous 1973 bestseller, *Subliminal Seduction* (which argued that, if you studied the highball glasses in liquor ads hard enough, you'd see all kinds of filthy messages hidden in the ice cubes), Wertham reproduced comic book panels that purported to show sexually suggestive images concealed in supposedly innocuous drawings. He also charged Wonder Woman with being the leader of a lesbian gang and denounced the Batman–Robin ménage as a pederast's wish-fulfillment fantasy. (Superman was spared any accusations of sexual impropriety, though Wertham did condemn the Man of Steel as a fascist who sported an abbreviated version of the Nazi SS insignia on his chest.)

Most sensational of all—and the feature that has made *Seduction of the Innocent* a coveted collectible among comic book aficionados—was a centerfold insert that reprinted the most gruesome illustrations Wertham could dig up, including a few—a woman having a hypodermic needle shoved into her eye, a baseball game played with dismembered human body parts—that, thanks to their appearance in *Seduction,* have achieved legendary status in the realm of comicdom.

The great juvenile delinquency scare of the early 1950s led to the creation of a U.S. Senate Subcommittee to investigate the phenomenon, at whose hearings—headed by Senator Estes Kefauver—Wertham was a star witness. Though lacking the high drama of the Army-McCarthy inquiry, the Kefauver hearings did provide some deliciously comic moments, most famously the testimony of William C. Gaines, publisher of the then-notorious (and now much-revered) line of EC horror comics, *Tales from the Crypt, The Vault of Horror,* and *The Haunt of Fear,* along with other "shock," crime, and combat titles. In one priceless exchange, Kefauver and his witness got into a debate over exactly what constituted "good taste" in a horror comic, with Kefauver flaunting the cover of *Crime SuspenStories* No. 22—which showed an ax murderer grasping his bloody weapon in one hand and a severed female head in the other—while Gaines insisted that the picture was, in fact, a model of artistic restraint for a comic book. "Bad taste," he earnestly explained, "might be defined as holding the head a little higher so that the neck could be seen dripping blood."[4]

To stave off the governmental censorship that was about to be visited upon them, comic book publishers formulated a set of ethics modeled on the infamous Hays Code that Hollywood had adopted as a self-protective measure in the 1930s when movies came under a similar attack. Addressed largely to issues of sex and violence in crime and horror comics, the code spelled out a list of general standards that, as far as the average reader was concerned, eliminated all the good stuff, specifically prohibiting "excessive and unnecessary knife and gun play" as well as any scene "dealing with walking dead, vampires and vampirism, ghouls, cannibalism, and werewolfism."

The "Shudder" Pulps

•

The crime and horror comics that caused so much commotion in the 1950s were the successors of another pop genre that, in its heyday, provoked its own explosion of moral outrage: the pulps. These garish, cheaply made publications—whose name derived from the crude, wood-pulp paper they were printed on—originated in 1896, quickly supplanting the dime novel as the sensational reading matter of choice for millions of ordinary Americans. By the 1920s, newsstands across the country were carrying upwards of two

hundred titles and selling more than ten million copies a month.

For several decades, the major categories of the pulps were ro-

(continued)

mance, crime and detective, western, and action-adventure (sea, air, jungle, war, and so on). Except for the first, all of them specialized in two-fisted, gun-blazing action. In 1933—after attending a performance in Paris at the Théâtre du Grand-Guignol—a young New York City publisher named Henry Steeger was inspired to convert his pulp detective magazine, *Dime Mystery,* into a publication dedicated to gory tales of Gothic horror in which virginal females were subjected to the most fiendish imaginable tortures, all lovingly described in graphic detail. The formula proved an immediate success, spawning dozens of imitators, among them *Startling Mystery, Thrilling Mystery, Eerie Mysteries, Horror Stories, Sinister Stories, Terror Tales,* and *Uncanny Tales.*

The term by which these gruesomely titillating magazines came to be known first appeared in an attack published in the April 1938 *American Mercury,* where a critic named Bruce Henry referred to them as "shudder" magazines and declared that the average issue contained "enough illustrated sex perversion to give Krafft-Ebing the unholy jitters."[5] While this claim

was somewhat hyperbolic, sex and sadism were, indeed, the major selling point of of the shudder pulps, as this typical passage from a story called "Girls for the Pain Dance" amply illustrates:

The madman paid no heed to the screams. One gloved hand twisted into the sheer fabric of the torn frock at Delia's throat. He ripped it down, baring the soft ablescent contours of her breasts to his maggot-brained tampering. "Don't, please don't!" Delia strained against the leather straps that bound her wrists and ankles. But the fiend persisted inexorably in his purpose. Pulling the glove off his right hand, he thrust his fingers through the steel rings of the hypodermic cylinder, set his palm against the extended plunger. For a second he pawed at the trembling body of the girl. Then viciously, he thrust the needle deep into her milk white flesh. Delia screamed again as the dread virus entered her body.[6]

The titles of the stories were deliciously lurid: "Enslaved to Satan," "House of the Doomed Brides," "The Pool Where Horror

(continued)

Dwelt," "Inn of the Shadow-Creatures," "Slaves of the Dancing Death," "Dance of the Beast People," "Flesh for the Devil's Piper," "The Corpse Marathon," "When it Rained Corpses." Even more important to the prurient appeal of the shudder pulps were the slick, often beautifully rendered covers—"macabre masterpieces," as the comic book artist and pop historian James Steranko describes them, "of mad scientists brandishing surgical instruments, hunchbacked assistants clutching hypodermics, animated cadavers and slimy scaly grotesqueries that lurked, leered, and lusted at half-nude lovelies, strapped to operating tables."[7] Mere words can't convey the sheer creepiness of the cover of *Horror Stories* (September 1935), which shows a demented clown sewing a decapitated head onto the shoulder of a lovely young woman in order to turn her into a two-headed sideshow freak. Or of *Dime Mystery* (August 1937), which depicts a scantily clad beauty about to be bisected by what appears to be an oversized paper trimmer, operated by the hideously deformed assistant of a crazed scientist. Or of *Dime Detective* (September 1935) in which a handsome guy (for a change) is being roasted alive on an open spit by a trio of evil Orientals (the only variety of Asian acknowledged by the pulps).

Fortunately, words aren't necessary, since these and many other examples can be viewed in volumes like Frank Robinson and Lawrence Davidson's *Pulp Culture: The Art of Fiction Magazines* (Collectors Press, 1998) and Peter Haining's *The Classic Era of American Pulp Magazines* (Chicago Review Press, 2000)—the pulps having gone the same route of so many once-vilified forms of American pop ephemera: i.e., from insidious trash to the subject of art books, scholarly tomes, and museum exhibitions.

Wertham's crusade produced some tangible results. It killed off hundreds of titles and decimated the comic book industry, driving scores of publishers out of business. Gaines and his EC collaborators managed to survive by scrapping their controversial crime and horror line and pouring their manic energies into a new satiric title, *MAD*.

Baby boomers tantalized (and deliciously terrified) by glimpses of their older sibling's issues of *Tales from The Crypt* and *The Vault of Horror* grew up to become avid collectors of these once-contraband items. And pop creators like George Romero and Stephen King—whose imaginations were shaped by their boyhood exposure to the taboo thrills of horror comics—were inspired to turn out their own homages to the EC tradition, like *Night of the Living Dead* and *Creepshow.*

One thing that the anticomics crusade had no effect on at all was the rate of juvenile violence, which actually rose during the latter years of the 1950s and throughout the 1960s. There should be nothing surprising about this fact. In hindsight, blaming juvenile delinquency on the comics seems as silly as blaming the sexual revolution of the 1920s on the Charleston (as some Jazz-Age bluenoses actually did). Nevertheless (like the troglodyte neighbor in Robert Frost's "Mending Wall" who can only mindlessly repeat the antiquated beliefs of his father), we are still stuck in the same hidebound mindset, substituting action films and video games for horror and crime comics and listening to various social scientists—Wertham's missionary heirs—who trot out highly questionable findings that are trumpeted in the national news, sending the parents of America into a wholly unjustified tizzy over their offsprings' addiction to the *Matrix* movies and *Wolfenstein 3D.*

Ever since July 2000, for example—when the American Medical Association, the American Academy of Pediatrics, the American Psychiatric Association, the American Psychological Association, the American Academy of Family Physicians, and the American Academy of Child and Adolescent Psychiatry issued a joint statement claiming that several thousand studies had unequivocally shown a direct link between between media violence and juvenile aggression—it has become, as Stephen Pinker writes, an article of faith "among conservative politicians and liberal health professionals alike . . . that violence in the media is a major cause of American violent crime."[8] But plenty of experts have have called those findings into serious question. Pinker refers to the psychologist Jonathan Freedman, for example, who discovered that contrary to the claims of the joint statement, only *two hundred studies* have looked for a connection between media violence and violent behavior and *more than half* failed to find one. The others found correlations that are small and readily explainable in other ways—for example, that violent children seek out violent entertainment, and that children are temporarily aroused (but not permanently affected) by action-packed footage. Freedman and several other psychologists who have reviewed the literature have concluded that exposure to media violence has little or no effect on violent behavior in the world. Reality checks from recent history suggest the same thing. People were more violent in the centuries *before* television and movies were invented. Canadians watch the same television shows as Americans but have a fourth their homicide rate. When the British colony of St. Helena installed television for the first time in 1995, its people did not become more violent. Violent computer games took off in the 1990s, a time when crime rates plummeted.[9]

Best-selling author and child psychologist Jonathan Kellerman puts the matter even more succinctly in *Savage Spawn,* a study of juvenile psychopathology. "Not a single causal link between media violence and criminality has ever been produced," Kellerman flatly declares—a view corroborated by many other experts in the fields of pediatrics, psychology, media studies, and forensics, and expounded upon at length in two highly persuasive books, Jib Fowles's *The Case* for *Television Violence* and Gerard Jones's *Killing Monsters: Why Children Need Fantasy, Super Heroes, and Make-Believe Violence.*[10] Jones does a particularly good job of casting doubt on the claims of alarmists:

> In the late 1960s, as crime rates were rising and the war in Vietnam preoccupied us, a groundswell of sentiment against violent entertainment actually succeeded in profoundly altering the landscape of children's culture. With help from the Federal Communications Commission and the grudging cooperation of the networks, groups such as Action for Children's Television succeeded in chasing most

of the violence out of kids' programming. The generation of cartoons created during the 1970s, from *The Smurfs* to *Strawberry Short-cake*, were designed to emphasize pro-social values and eschew slapstick humor and physical contact. . . . Prime-time action shows like *The Incredible Hulk* and *The Dukes of Hazzard* featured little action and not a single instance of bodily harm. The mighty Hulk had to content himself with tearing the bumpers off cars, smashing through doors, and sometimes knocking a bad guy into a swimming pool. . . .

We tend to forget now, but for about a decade not very long ago, we truly did give our children the nearly violence-free popular culture that so many critics of the media are pressing for now. . . . What happened during those years? Crime rates increased. Our national anxiety about violence, as measured by opinion polls, worsened. The kids who spent their formative years in that pop-cultural milieu became the teenagers of the mid-1980s, when crime rates rose again. The kids who spent their formative years in the 1980s, on the other hand, when action-packed movies, TV shows, video games, and combat toys seemed to be taking over kid culture, became the teenagers of the late 1990s, when those rates plummeted. Obviously, the Smurfs were no more responsible for the crime wave of the 1980s than the Teenage Mutant Ninja Turtles were for the relative calm that followed.[11]

As Jones and like-minded critics demonstrate, virtually all the studies that purport to show a link between exposure to media violence and aggressive behavior are afflicted with significant problems, ranging from methodological flaws to bizarre assumptions about the way the human imagination processes and makes use of fantasy. To begin with, they tend to be conducted under highly artificial conditions that bear no resemblance to a child's actual day-to-day experience. "The youngster views footage quite unlike what he's seen at home: violent scenes snipped out of a show without a story to make sense of it, humor to relieve it, or the dramatic closure that ends nearly every TV show," Jones points out. "Then he is told to play with the other kids, all strangers, all under stress, while the researchers watch." One famous study concluded that—because its preschooler subjects became "three times more aggressive" after being forced to watch a video of *Mr. Rogers' Neighborhood*—TV viewing itself, regardless of content, incites violent behavior. As Jones sensibly notes, however, it is equally likely that the results simply prove that young kids don't like to be ordered around by strange adults and told what to watch on TV.[12]

What researchers mean by "aggression" is another problem. Typically, a social scientist (often a middle-aged man who has evidently forgotten how much joy he took as a kid from running around and shooting at his buddies with a Marshal Dillon cap pistol or a spark-spewing *Star Trek* zap gun) will solemnly report that, after viewing an episode of *Teenage Mutant Ninja Turtles,* his third-grade male subjects began to leap around and administer make-believe karate chops and flying kicks to each other. His conclusion: watching video "violence" incites juvenile aggression. What is missing from this pronouncement—besides fundamental common sense—is the recognition that there is an enormous difference between real aggression that is meant to inflict harm on another person and the kind of rough-and-tumble horseplay that young males have gleefully engaged in from the inception of the species. Jones refers to a well-known study from 1963 "which showed that children who had watched films of someone punching an inflatable clown doll subsequently punched an identical clown doll more often than children who had not"—a finding that, as Jones suggests, might have unnerving implications if you're an inflatable clown but hardly says anything meaningful about the link between cinematic violence and juvenile aggression.[13]

There's no doubt that, for young boys, there's a connection between watching action-packed entertainment and roughhousing. That was certainly true of me and all the other nice, middle-class Bronx-born boomers I grew up with. After watching a few hours of *Wild Bill Hickock* or *The Cisco Kid,* we could hardly contain ourselves. We would strap on our leatherette holsters and leap into action, galloping around the house on invisible steeds, taking potshots at each other with our Hopalong Cassidy pistols, throwing ourselves at each other and wrestling like bear cubs. The cries of our mothers—shouting at us (in those pre-PC days) to go play outside if we wanted to act like "wild Indians"—still echoes in my ears.

That the well-behaved little boys who turn into karate-chopping dervishes after sitting through their favorite action cartoons are actually engaged in normal physical play and not rehearsing for careers as serial killers is a truism which every levelheaded parent recognizes, however much of it has eluded the understanding of the "experts." There have, of course, been welcome exceptions—social scientists who acknowledge the all-important difference between rowdy play and real aggression. Jeffrey Goldstein, for example—a communications professor at the University of Utrecht—not only emphasizes this distinction but explains how the failure to acknowledge it leads to serious misconceptions about juvenile male behavior:

> Sometimes, I accompany teachers to the playground during recess to watch elementary-school children at play. Boys are seen running, chasing, pretending to shoot one another or to be shot, or they stand face-to-face as they go through martial arts movements. Girls, more often than not, do not participate in this highly active, raucous, almost anarchic play. Instead, they stand mostly in small groups talking animatedly, their conversations punctuated by shrieks and laughter. When asked to describe what they see, the teachers invariably say that the boys are aggressive and the girls are "nice" and not aggressive.
>
> In many respects, the boys' play resembles real aggression, which also involves running, chasing, and fleeing. But there are differences between play fighting and real fighting, notably in facial expression, the longer duration and repetition of play fighting, and the fact that the boys remain together once these play episodes have run their

course. The main difference—the defining feature of aggression, which is absent from aggressive play—is the intent to injure another person.

The boys recognize these differences and are cognizant that they are playing, not fighting. In fact, if some boys fail to observe this distinction—fighting while their counterparts are pretending to fight—they will be excluded from subsequent play. . . .

The girls standing and chatting on the playground, in contrast to the boys whose play is more active, may be engaged in aggression if their behavior is designed to hurt someone. Social ostracism and gossip are often used by girls to hurt other girls, and thus constitute a form of aggressive behavior. What at first appears to be aggressive boys and nonaggressive girls may, in deed and in consequence, be the other way around.[14]

Few people who have raised sons and daughters would argue with Goldstein's observations. Every such parent knows that, between the ages of, say, ten and sixteen, boys—though far more likely to wreck the living room while play-wrestling with their pals—are, as a general rule, much less cruel than girls: far less likely to engage in—or be victimized by—the kind of sadistic social behavior that causes real emotional damage. Your son might come home from a schoolyard scuffle with a shiner, but your daughter is the one who's more likely to be traumatized because her former best friends have cut her out of their clique and are now spreading malicious gossip about her behind her back.

This is not to say that the occasional deeply disturbed adolescent or prepubescent male might not commit a terrible act after seeing something violent on TV. But such cases are extreme anomalies, played up on the evening news for the same reason that a couple of atypical shark attacks on the Florida coast are instantly transformed into a national *Jaws*-like crisis that spoils summer vacation for beachgoers everywhere: i.e., because the news media profits by playing on the free-floating anxieties of the public.[15] The fact that an unstable little boy (or girl) might emulate a televised crime clearly proves nothing beyond the fact that deeply disturbed people don't respond like the rest of us. (There's a famous Charles Addams cartoon showing a theaterful of moviegoers, all weeping copious tears as they stare at the screen—except for the Uncle Fester character, who is cackling merrily.) Should the Beatles' *White Album* be banned because its songs—especially "Helter Skelter"—inspired Charles Manson to perpetrate his atrocities? Or *The Catcher in the Rye* be removed from bookshelves because the assassin of John Lennon identified with Holden Caulfield? Or Cecil B. DeMille's *The Ten Commandments* be purged from the airwaves because, in 1959, a German psychopath named Pommerencke butchered several women after watching the faithless female Israelites wantonly disport themselves at the feet of the Golden Calf?

The notion that little boys are sweet, docile creatures until taught otherwise by the media can only be seriously entertained by someone who has never witnessed or experienced a phenomenon common in certain liberal communities: the sight of, say, a three-year-old boy—raised in a household where violent toys are forbidden and the most action-packed TV program he is permitted to watch is *SpongeBob SquarePants*—spontaneously picking up a twig or Popsicle stick and wielding it as a weapon in a make-believe swordfight with a playmate. As Stephen Pinker points out, "children are violent well before they have been infected by war toys or cultural stereotypes. The most violent age is not adolescence but toddlerhood; in a recent large study, almost half the boys just past the age of two, and a slightly smaller percentage of girls, engaged in hitting, biting, and kicking."[16] Though there will always be those who deny it, we belong to an innately violent species, one of whose defining features is that "aboriginal capacity for murderous excitement" described by William James.

Moreover, if young people are so easily seduced and manipulated by media images—if there is, as the self-appointed moral sentries imply, a simple monkey-see, monkey-do relationship between the pop entertainment adolescents consume and their daily behavior—then why, one might legitimately ask, aren't teenagers *nicer*? "If young Americans have seen tens of thousands of murders on TV," writes

Barry Glassner, "surely they have seen even more acts of kindness. On sitcoms, romantic comedies, movies of the week, soaps, medical dramas, and even on police shows, people are constantly falling in love and helping each other out. The characters on most prime-time shows share so much peace, tolerance and understanding that you might even call it 'gratuitous harmony'."[17] During the 1980s, when juvenile crime rates were on the rise, the biggest phenomenon on national TV was *The Cosby Show,* a program that, if anything, promoted family values to a fault. Contrary to accusations that they "glorify violence," even hyperkinetic action shows and movies reinforce traditional morality, vilifying the bad guys and celebrating the triumph of virtue. Indeed, if the average Hollywood shoot-'em-up can be criticized for anything, it is for portraying a universe devoid of moral ambiguity, where evil is easily identified and invariably defeated, and the all-American heroes are saints armed with semi-automatic weapons—a view of the world that is, arguably, more insidious than all the cinematic havoc and choreographed carnage.

For the most part, video games also traffic in old-fashioned good-guy, bad-guy fantasies. The argument that they are dangerously realistic is simply silly, since their meticulously designed action sequences are, in the words of Jib Fowles, "as stylized as the swordplay in Japanese Noh theater."[18] (The same, incidentally, is true of the violence in such once-controversial, now-classic works as *The Wild Bunch* and *Bonnie and Clyde.* It is worth noting that—despite the clichéd claim that movies have become intolerably violent—nothing coming out of Hollywood today compares to the grueling level of bloodshed in these and other Vietnam-era films.)

The other charge commonly made against video games—that they are far more insidious than old-fashioned juvenile pastimes because they are more "interactive"—holds equally little water. Nothing was more interactive than the "violent" play of my own 1950s boyhood, when our targets were not animated pixels but live human beings who would shoot back at us with cap pistols, dart guns, ping-pong-ball rifles, and rubber-tipped arrows. If there's one legitimate complaint that parents can make about video games, it is that they are not *active* enough. They are too sedentary. They don't encourage kids to run around outdoors and shoot each other in the healthy way we did in the past.

Indeed, there is a baffling failure on the part of the "experts" to recognize not merely the physical but the psychological benefits of violent pastimes for children. This was certainly true of Frederic Wertham, who might have been expected to know better. As psychoanalysis teaches, one of the primary functions of horror stories is to help the audience manage its unspoken fears—cope with profoundly disturbing experiences—by giving them a reassuring narrative shape. Even more than A-bomb worries, the constant barrage of horrific death camp revelations, in both words and pictures, was a source of intolerable anxiety for countless Americans in the early 1950s, including very young ones who—as I can attest from personal experience— could not help but be traumatized by the ghastly images of Nazi atrocities that regularly showed up in everything from *Life* magazine to Saturday matinee newsreels. Surely it is no accident that nearly all the major figures involved in the creation of Wertham's most famous target—the EC horror comics—were Jewish, nor that the characteristic fantasy of *Tales from the Crypt* and its sister publications was the rotting corpse rising from the grave to take revenge on its murderer. For both creators and readers, in short, these unassuming publications were a way—however, unconscious—of purging a sanity-threatening nightmare by turning it into a comprehensible story with an emotionally satisfying climax.

Wertham got one thing right, at least. The horror comics of the 1950s were excessively graphic and grisly. Indeed, for all the assaults on contemporary pop culture, it is impossible to conceive of any current day kiddie entertainment approaching the grotesque violence of this typical EC story cited during the Kefauver hearings:

An extremely sadistic schoolteacher gives special attention to one of her pupils in order to curry favor with the boy's rich, widowed father. In a year, she succeeds in marrying the man, but he turns out to be a miser. She stabs him to death with a butcher knife approximately a foot and a half in length and three inches wide. The picture shows the body of the old man, limbs askew, falling to the floor, emitting a gurgle. There is a large hole in his back and blood is squirting in all directions. The wife is behind him clutching the bloody butcher knife. She says, "You stupid old fool! I've stood for your miserly penny-pinching ways long enough! From now on it'll be my money . . . and I'll spend it my way! Die, Ezra . . . die!" She then covers up her crime by throwing him into a pen with a wild bull that gores his body to pieces. She now has the money, but also the stepson whom she hates. The boy suspects that she killed his father and makes her chase him around the farm by calling her names. He leads her to some quicksand and she falls in. Several pictures show her as she begs the boy to get help. He promises to do so if she confesses to him that she killed his father. She does so, and he then her lets her sink to her death. A closeup is shown of the terrified woman, sunk into the quicksand which is flowing into her open mouth.[19]

By the same token, of course, it is impossible to conceive of America's best-loved action hero—Indiana Jones, say—proving his prowess by shooting off the ears of a cat, as Davy Crockett does in this 1840 tale, in which he engages in a marksmanship contest with his archrival Mike Fink:

So one night I fell in with him in the woods, where him and his wife shook down a blanket for me in his wigwam. In the morning sez Mike to me, "I've got the handsomest wife and the fastest horse and the sharpest shooting-iron in all Kentuck, and if any man dare doubt it, I'll be in his hair quicker than hell can scorch a feather." This put my dander up and I sez, "I've nothing to say agin your wife, Mike, for it can't be denied she's a shocking handsome woman, and Mrs. Crockett's in Tennessee, and I've got no horses.

Now Mike, I don't exactly like to tell you you lie about what you say about your rifle, but I'm damned if you speak the truth, and I'll prove it. Do you see that there cat sitting on the top rail of your potato patch, about a hundred and fifty yards off? If she ever hears again, I'll be shot if it shan't be without ears." So I blazed away and I'll bet you a horse, the ball cut off both the old tom cat's ears close to his head, and shaved the hair clean across the skull, as slick as if I'd done it with a razor, and the critter never stirred nor knew he'd lost his ears till he tried to scratch 'em."[20]

The point is that—while American popular culture is far more technologically sophisticated than it used to be—it is not, by any stretch, more brutal. Nor, despite the common belief to the contrary, is our country plagued with a higher incidence of violent crime. While the news media has a vested interest in whipping up mass hysteria—as Barry Glassner makes abundantly clear in his indispensable book, *The Culture of Fear*—the truth is that homicide rates have been steadily declining in this country for two decades. According to the FBI Uniform Crime Report, there were 10.2 murders per one hundred thousand people in 1980. By the year 2000 that number had plunged to 5.5.[21] Even during the height of the hysteria prompted by the Columbine massacre, a study conducted by the National Center for Education Statistics showed that there had been no significant increase in violent crimes at U.S. schools for two decades.[22]

The general assumption that American popular culture is uniquely violent is also simply wrong. Anyone who doubts this assertion is invited to familiarize himself with the rich tradition of Italian gore movies like *Cannibal Holocaust, Zombie Flesh Eaters,* and *The Gestapo's Last Orgy.* Or with the pop culture of Japan, where kiddie comics routinely portray every imaginable atrocity from beheading to disembowelment; where a popular filmmaker—Takashi Miike—makes movies so grisly that when *Ichi the Killer* was shown at the 2003 Toronto Film Festival, airplane vomit bags were handed out to audience members; and where a convicted cannibal named Issei Sagawa—

who killed, butchered, and ate his German girlfriend while studying in Paris in 1981—has become a national celebrity, bestselling author, weekly newspaper columnist, and staple on television talk shows.[23] Even France is turning out more disturbingly violent movies than America these days. According to film provocateur Gaspar Noé, his nearly unwatchably brutal film *Irreversible*—which features a nine-minute rape sequence so sickeningly graphic that several audience members had to be treated with oxygen at a screening in Cannes—was partly created as "an antidote to Hollywood's slick and increasingly prettified violence."[24]

Can it really be that so many specialists in the area of media violence are so utterly mistaken? That the truth—as Jean de la Bruyère says in the epigram I quoted earlier—is "the exact contrary of what is generally believed?" Paradoxically, the sheer quantity of violent action and shocking horror in popular culture may be a reflection, not of how savage we are as a people, but of the reverse—how civilized we've become. Certainly this is a theory advanced by various experts, like the sociologists Norbert Elias and Eric Dunning—who speak of the "the quest for excitement in unexciting societies." Alfred Hitchcock, another person who knew something about these matters, similarly remarked in a 1936 interview: "I am out to give the public good, healthy mental shake-ups. Civilization has become so screening and sheltering that we cannot experience sufficient thrills at first hand. Therefore, to prevent our becoming sluggish and jellified, we have to experience them artificially, and the screen is the best media for this."[25] It can be argued that this unprecedented refinement of our sensibilities—our inhabiting a society where (unless you are forced to watch a PETA propaganda tape) it is entirely possible to go through life without seeing so much as a chicken get beheaded—is precisely what has caused such widespread finickiness when it comes even to fake violence.

In May 2003, Martin Rees—Britain's Royal Astronomer and one of the world's most esteemed cosmologists—came out with a highly publicized book called *Our Final Hour,* in which he gives civilization as we know it only a fifty-fifty chance of surviving the present century. If Rees's worst-case predictions are correct, it won't be media violence that does us in. It seems highly unlikely, for example, that the apocalyptic tendencies of aspiring bioterrorists have been shaped by overexposure to *Resident Evil*. Let us hope that Rees is wrong and that our children grow up to enjoy the kind of future that—prior to 9/11—America seemed to heading for: a place where real-life violence was on a steady decline and the video games just kept getting cooler.

Robert Redford— Cannibal Psychopath?

•

The current crusade against violent pop entertainment is based on the assumption that crime (particularly among juveniles) is out of control in this country. But is this assumption true? The short answer is—*no*. As Barry Glassner points out in his book, *The Culture of Fear*, statistics prove that there's been a "steep drop in youth crime throughout the 1990s," reaching "a record low during the 1997 school year (19 deaths out of 54 million children)."

But what about phenomena like mass and serial murder? Surely, the epidemic of such terrifying crimes is a sign of "societal rot."

Again, this a wholly erroneous perception. First, serial killers are hardly running rampant in this country. The FBI estimates that there are perhaps fifty of them on the loose at any time. That's fifty too many, of course, but still a statistically negligible number in a population of 275 million. And most serial murderers are the sort of squalid little sex fiends (as they used to be called) who've always preyed on hookers. The average middle-class person—who probably worries most about crossing paths with a serial killer—has the least to fear.

It's also important to realize that the kind of homicidal maniacs we now call serial killers have always existed in America—and probably in more abundance than they do nowadays. The case of John Johnson is instructive.

Johnson was among the most colorful of the nineteenth-century

(continued)

mountain men—those lone adventurers who braved the rigors of the great Western wilderness to trap beaver, trade fur, and live free of civilization. His gravestone and a single daguerreotype portrait are the only physical traces of his existence that still remain. But we know a fair amount about him, thanks to a historian named Raymond Thorpe who interviewed a number of old-timers who had crossed paths with Johnson years before.

A sullen, surly brute of a man, Johnson was as skilled at scalping Indians as he was at skinning beaver. Throughout his career, he collected hundreds of these grisly trophies. Though he sold most of them for bounties, he never parted with the dried scalp of the first Arapaho he killed, sporting it on his belt as an ornament.

What really made his reputation, however, was his taste for human flesh. Following the killing of his wife by a party of Crow Indians, Johnson launched a one-man vendetta against the tribe. Over the next few years, he slaughtered Crow warriors by the dozen, carving up their corpses and eating their livers raw. Before long, he had acquired the nickname by which he would forever be known among his contemporaries: "Liver-Eating" Johnson (or sometimes just "The Liver–Eater").

In one notorious incident, he and a bunch of cohorts massacred a band of thirty-two Sioux Indians camped by a river. Then—after commemorating the occasion by devouring his favorite body part—Johnson superintended as his companions decapitated the corpses, boiled down the skulls, mounted them on poles, and planted them along the riverbank for the benefit of gawking steamboat passengers. Escapades like this made Johnson a figure of awe and admiration among his fellow mountain men—a living legend.

The life and deeds of "The Liver–Eater" are an example of something we tend to overlook in our own violence-obsessed times. Bloodshed and mayhem were no less endemic to American society a hundred years ago than they are today. On the contrary. The history of the American frontier—with its appalling record of lynchings, massacres, shootings, and other everyday barbarities—makes our own

(continued)

time seem like a Golden Age. One big difference between the past and the present is that, back in the days of John Johnson, people with particularly savage tendencies could find various socially approved outlets for their behavior. They might even be rewarded for it. A man with a taste for human blood could travel out west and satisfy his cravings to his heart's content—as long as he vented his sadism on "redskins."

Nowadays, a man who slaughters a succession of strangers, butchers their bodies, and dines on their flesh is called a serial killer. But a hundred years ago—because his victims weren't white—a man like "Liver-Eating" Johnson was called something else. He was called a hero.

Now, it so happens that, in 1972, Johnson's life was turned a slick Hollywood movie called *Jeremiah Johnson,* starring Robert Redford in the title role. There's plenty of killing in the movie, but it's all very bloodless and sanitized—the kind of acrobatic, frontier action that little boys have thrilled to since the heyday of Tom Mix. And needless to say, there's not a hint of cannibalism in it.

So the question is: when was life in America really more brutal? A hundred years ago, when public hangings were a popular form of family entertainment—when the corpses of slain outlaws and lynching victims were proudly displayed in public squares—and when a sadistic killer like "Liver-Eating" Johnson was celebrated in story and song? Or today, when most of us would flinch at the sight of a freshly butchered farm animal, and when the only violence we permit ourselves to enjoy is, by and large, virtual—perpetrated against celluloid villains and the computerized images on video screens?

NOTES

•

CHAPTER ONE

1. Leslie Fiedler, *What was Literature?: Class Culture and Mass Society* (New York: Simon and Schuster, 1982), p. 50.

2. Hervey Allen, *Israfel: The Life and Times of Edgar Allan Poe* (New York: Farrar & Rinehart. 1934), p. 408.

3. Quote by Ann Douglas in *Terrible Honesty: Mongrel Manhattan in the 1920s* (New York: Farrar, Straus and Giroux, 1995), p. 169.

4. "Monday Night Hunters," *Cornell Magazine*, November/December 1997, p. 44.

5. Sigmund Freud, *Civilization and Its Discontents,* trans. Joan Riviere (London, 1930; rpt. New York: Dover, 1994), p. 40.

6. See poem number 670, *The Complete Poems of Emily Dickinson,* ed. Thomas H. Johnson (Boston: Little, Brown, 1955), p. 333.

7. Fiedler, *What was Literature?*, p. 50.

8. *Danse Macabre* (New York: Everest House, 1981), p. 175.

9. *Studies in Classic American Literature* (New York: 1924; rpt. New York: Viking, 1964), p. 10.

10. The Gomme quote is cited by Alan Dundes in *The Study of Folklore* (Englewood Cliffs, N.J.: Prentice-Hall, 1965), p. 95. The Panofsy quote is from his essay, "Style and Medium in Motion Pictures," reprinted in *Awake in the Dark,* David Denby, ed. (New York: Vintage Books, 1977), p. 33.

11. *The Hard Facts of the Grimms' Fairy Tales* (Princeton: Princeton University Press, 1987), p. 198.

12. Ted Robert Gurr, "Historical Trends in Violent Crimes: A Critical Review of the Evidence," in *Crime and Justice: An Annual Review of Research,* ed. Michael Tonry and Norval Morris (Chicago: University of Chicago Press, 1981), p. 312.

CHAPTER TWO

1. G. Legman, *Love and Death: A Study in Censorship* (New York: Hacker Art Books, 1949), pp. 30, 31–32.

2. Margaret Dalziel, *Popular Fiction 100 Years Ago: An Unexplored Tract of Literary History* (London: Cohen & West, 1957), p. xxi.

3. "'Cops and Robbers' Leads to Policy Review," *New York Times*, 6 April 2000, Sec. B, p. 4.

4. *Maverick, The Restless Gun, Wells Fargo, Cheyenne, Wyatt Earp, Wagon Train, Colt .45, Trackdown, Have Gun Will Travel, Gunsmoke, The Lawman, The Texan, The Rifleman, Bat Masterson, Yancy Derringer, Wanted: Dead or Alive, Cimarron City.*

CHAPTER THREE

1. Reprinted in *The Tall Tales of Davy Crockett: The Second Nashville Series of Crockett Almanacs 1839–1841*, ed. Michael A. Lofaro (Knoxville, Tenn.: University of Tennessee Press, 1987), p. 18.

2. Edmund Pearson, *Dime Novels* (Boston: Little Brown, 1929), p. 46.

3. Russel Nye, *The Unembarrassed Muse* (New York: The Dial Press, 1970), pp. 204–205.

4. Raymond L. Andrews, "Grandfather Liked Them Gory," *Esquire*, Feb. 1950, p. 57.

5. Edward Ellis, *Seth Jones, or, The Captives of the Frontier*, reprinted in *Popular American Fiction: Dime Novels*, ed. Philip Durham (New York: The Odyssey Press, 1966), pp. 64–65.

6. Michael Anglo, *Penny Dreadfuls and Other Victorian Horrors* (London: Jupiter, 1987), p. 26.

7. *See* E. S. Turner, *Boys Will Be Boys: The Story of Sweeney Todd, Deadwood Dick, Sexton Blaks, Billy Bunter, Dick Barton, etc.* (London: Michael Joseph, 1948), p. 37.

8. Peter Haining, *Sweeney Todd: The Real Story of the Demon Barber of Fleet Street* (London: Robson Books, 1993), p. 121.

9. Anglo, *Penny Dreadfuls*, p. 23.

10. Margaret Dalziel, *Popular Fiction 100 Years Ago: An Unexplored Tract of Literary History* (London: Cohen & West, 1957), p. 20.

11. *See* Steven Starker, *Evil Influences: Crusades Against the Mass Media* (New Brunswick, N.J.: Transaction Publishers, 1989), p. 66, and Peter Haining, *The Art of Horror Stories* (London: Souvenir Press, 1976), p. 19.

CHAPTER FOUR

1. Jackson Morley, ed. *Crimes and Punishment: A Pictorial Encyclopedia of Aberrant Behavior* (London: BCP Publishing, 1974), Vol. 18, p. 107.

2. Daniel Gerould, *Guillotine: Its Legend and Lore* (New York: Blast Books, 1992), pp. 37–39.

3. Luc Sante, *Low Life: Lures and Snares of Old New York* (New York: Vintage, 1991), p. 206.

4. *See* Robert Collison, *The Story of Street Literature: Forerunner of the Popular Press* (Santa Barbara, Calif.: Clio Press, 1973), p. 38.

5. Charles Hindley, *Curiosities of Street Literature* (London: The Broadstreet King, 1966), Vol. II, p. 219.

6. *See* Victor E. Neuberg, *Popular Literature: A History and Guide: From the Beginning of Printing to the Year 1897* (New York: Penguin, 1977), p. 137.

7. Olive Woolley Burt, *American Murder Ballads and Their Stories* (New York: Oxford University Press, 1958), p. 27.

8. Harold W. Thompson, *Body, Boots, and Britches: Folktales, Ballads and Speech from Country New York* (Syracuse, N.Y.: Syracuse University Press, 1979), pp. 432–435.

9. Much of the information in this and the following paragraphs comes from David Reynolds, *Beneath the American Renaissance: The Subversive Imagination in the Age of Emerson and Melville* (New York: Knopf, 1988), pp. 173–177.

10. Quoted in Daneen Wardtop, *Emily Dickinson's Gothic: Goblin with a Gauge* (Iowa City: University of Iowa Press, 1996), pp. 7–8.

11. Karen Halttunen, *Murder Most Foul: The Killer and the American Gothic Imagination* (Cambridge, Mass.: Harvard University Press, 1998), pp. 73–75.

12. Leonard DeVries, *'Orrible Murder: Victorian Crime and Passion* (New York: Taplinger, 1971).

CHAPTER FIVE

1. Barbara Tuchman, *A Distant Mirror: The Calamitous 14th Century* (New York: Ballantine Books, 1978), p. 153.

2. Andrew McCall, *The Medieval Underworld* (London: Hamish Hamilton, 1979), pp. 72–76.

3. Jacobus de Viragine, *The Golden Legend: Readings on the Saints,* Vol. II, trans. William Granger Ryan (Princeton: Princeton University Press, 1993), pp. 265–66.

4. John Spalding Gatton, " 'There Must be Blood': Mutilation and Martyrdom on the Medieval Stage," in *Violence in Drama,* ed. James Redmond (Cambridge: Cambridge University Press, 1991), pp. 79–92.

5. Maurice Charney, "The Persuasiveness of Violence in Elizabethan Plays," in *Renaissance Drama: New Series II,* ed. S. Schoenbaum (Evanston, Ill.: Northwestern University Press, 1969), p. 60.

6. All passages from Seneca come from E. F. Watling's translation, *Seneca: Four Tragedies and Octavia* (London: Penguin, 1996). Used by permission.

7. Quoted in Huston Diehl, "The Iconography of Violence in English Renaissance Tragedy," in *Renaissance Drama: New Series XI,* ed. Douglas Cole (Evanston, Ill.: Northwestern University Press, 1980), p. 31.

8. See Mario Praz, *The Flaming Heart: Essays on Crashaw, Machiavelli, and Other Studies in the Relations between Italian and English Literature from Chaucer to T. S. Eliot* (Gloucester, Mass.: Peter Smith, 1966), p. 147.

9. Mel Gordon, *The Grand Guignol: Theatre of Fear and Terror* (New York: Amok Press, 1988), p. 47. Other sources used in this section are: Victor Emeljanow, "Grand-Guignol and the Orchestration of Violence," in *Violence in Drama,* ed. James Redmond (Cambridge: Cambridge University Press, 1991), pp. 151–163; John M. Callahan, "The Ultimate in Theatre Violence," in *Violence in Drama,* pp. 165–175; Agnès Pierron, "The House of Horrors," *Grand Street,* 57, No. 1 (1996), 87–100; and "Outdone by Reality," *Time* magazine, (30 November 1962), pp. 78, 80.

CHAPTER SIX

1. Michel Foucalt, *Discipline and Punish: The Birth of the Prison,* trans. Alan Sheridan (New York: Vintage Books, 1977), p. 3.

2. Geoffrey Abbott, *The Book of Execution: An Encyclopedia of Methods of Judicial Execution* (London: Headline Publishing, 1994), p. 37.

3. Roland Auguet, *Cruelty and Civilization: The Roman Games* (London: George Allen & Unwin, 1972), pp. 81, 86–87.

4. E. D. Cuming, "Blood Sport" in *The History of Popular Culture,* ed. Norman F. Cantor and Michael S. Werthman (New York: Macmillan, 1968), p. 298.

5. Gene Smith and Jane Barry Smith, *The Police Gazette* (New York: Simon & Schuster, 1972), p. 130.

6. Quoted by Cuming, p. 296.

7. Abbott, *The Book of Execution,* pp. 51–52.

8. Pieter Spierenberg, *The Spectacle of Suffering: Executions and the Evolution of Repression from a Preindustrial Metropolis to the European Experience* (Cambridge: Cambridge University Press, 1984), p. 112.

9. David D. Cooper, *The Lesson of the Scaffold: The Public Execution Controversy in Victorian England* (Athens, Ohio: Ohio University Press, 1974), p. 3.

10. Cooper, *The Lesson of the Scaffold,* p. 3.

11. Thomas W. Laqueur, "Crowds, carnival and the state in English executions, 1604–1868," in *The First Modern Society: Essay in History in Honour of Lawrence Stone,* ed. A. E. Beier, David Cannadine, and James M. Rosenheim (Cambridge: Cambridge University Press, 1989), p. 335.

12. Cooper, *The Lesson of the Scaffold,* p. 7.

13. Richard Zaks, *An Underground Education* (New York: Doubleday, 1997), p. 100.

14. Laqueur, "Crowds," p. 324.

15. Keith Hollingsworth, *The Newgate Novel 1830–1847: Bulwer, Ainsworth, Dickens & Thakery* (Detroit: Wayne State University Press, 1963), p. 304.

16. Abbott, *The Book of Execution,* p. 238.

17. Ibid., pp. 238–39.

18. F. Gonzalez-Crussi, *Suspended Animation: Six Essays on the Preservation of Bodily Parts* (New York: Harcourt Brace, 1995), pp. 49–50, 51–52.

19. Edmund Burke, *A Philosophical Enquiry into the Origin of Our Ideas of the Sublime and Beautiful.* (Oxford: Oxford University Press, 1990), p. 43.

CHAPTER SEVEN

1. Erwin Panofsky, "Style and Medium in the Motion Pictures," in *Awake in the Dark,* ed. David Denby (New York: Vintage Books, 1977), pp. 30–48.

2. Philip French, "Violence in the Cinema," *The Twentieth Century,* Winter 1964–1965, pp. 115–130.

3. Gerald Mast and Bruce Kawin, *A Short History of the Movies,* 8th Edition (New York: Longman, 2002), p. 39.

4. Mast and Kawin, *A Short History,* p. 40.

5. Quoted in David J. Skal, *The Monster Show: A Cultural History of Horror* (New York: W. W. Norton, 1993), p. 125.

6. Kevin Brownlow, *Behind the Mask of Innocence* (Berkeley: University of California, 1990), p. 168.

7. Quoted by James Twitchell, *Preposterous Violence: Fables of Aggression in Modern Culture* (New York: Oxford University Press, 1989), p. 169.

8. Introduction to E. S. Turner, *Boys Will Be Boys: The Story of Sweeney Todd, Deadwood Dick, Sexton Blake, Billy Bunter, Dick Bunter, Et Al.* (London: Michael Joseph, 1948), pp. 7–8.

9. Twitchell, *Preposterous Violence,* p. 86.

10. Ibid., p. 88.

11. *See* Steven Starker, *Evil Influences: Crusades Against the Mass Media* (New Brunswick, N.J.: 1989), p. 59.

12. Starker, *Evil Influences,* pp. 60–62.

13. Quoted in Starker, *Evil Influences,* p. 62.

14. American Tract Society, "Tract No. 515: Novel-Reading," reprinted in Paul C. Gutjahr, ed., *Popular American Literature of the 19th Century* (New York: Oxford University Press, 2001), p. 73.

15. American Tract Society, "Tract No. 493: Beware of Bad Books," Gutjahr, pp. 60–61.

16. Quoted in Michael Denning, *Mechanic Accents: Dime Novels and Working Class Culture in America* (New York: Verso, 1987), pp. 29–30.

17. See Harold Schechter, *Fiend: The Shocking True Story of America's Youngest Serial Killer* (New York: Simon & Schuster/Pocket Books, 2000), pp. 90–99.

18. Denning, p. 9.

19. All quotes in this paragraph come from Starker, pp. 75–76.

20. John K. Ryan, "Are the Comics Moral?" *Forum* 95 (1936), pp. 301–304.

21. All quotes come from Stephen Starker, *Evil Influences: Crusades Against the Mass Media* (New Brunswick, N.J.: 1989), p. 115–119.

22. John Houseman, "What Makes American Movies Tough?" *Vogue* (January 15, 1947), pp. 88, 120, 125).

23. Ibid., p. 120.

24. G. Legman, *Love & Death: A Study in Censorship* (New York: Hacker Art Books, 1949), p. 34.

25. Ibid, pp. 50–51.

26. Fiedler, *What was Literature?* p. 50 (see chap 1, n. 1).

27. George Stade, review of Wendy Lesser's *Pictures at an Execution, New York Times Book Review,* December 1, 1994, p. 10.

CHAPTER EIGHT

1. James Gilbert, *Cycle of Outrage: America's Reaction to the Juvenile Delinquent in the 1950s* (New York: Oxford University Press, 1986), p. 63.

2. Ibid., pp. 68–69.

3. Ibid., pp. 100–101.

4. See Frank Jacobs, *The Mad World of William M. Gaines* (Secaucus, N.J.: Lyle Stuart, 1972), pp. 108–109.

5. Quoted in Peter Haining, *The Classic Era of American Pulp Magazines* (Chicago: Chicago Review Press, 2000), p. 135.

6. Ibid.

7. James Steranko, *The Steranko History of Comics,* Volume One (Reading, Penn.: Supergraphics, 1970), p. 27.

8. Stephen Pinker, *The Blank Slate: The Modern Denial of Human Nature* (New York: Viking, 2002), p. 311.

9. Ibid.

10. Jonathan Kellerman, *Savage Spawn: Reflections of Violent Children* (New York: Ballantine, 1999), p. 72. Jib Fowles, *The Case for Television Violence* (Thousand Oaks, Calif.: Sage Publications, 1999). Gerard Jones, *Killing Monsters: Why Children Need Fantasy, Super Heroes, and Make-Believe Violence* (New York: Basic Books, 2002).

11. Gerard Jones, *Killing Monsters*, pp. 41–43.

12. Ibid, pp. 34–35.

13. Ibid., p. 38.

14. Jeffrey Goldstein, "Immortal Kombat: Toys and Violent Video Games," in *Why We Watch: The Attractions of Violent Entertainment,* ed. Jeffey H. Goldstein (New York: Oxford University Press, 1998), p. 54.

15. For an incisive exploration of this phenomenon, *see* Barry Glassner, *The Culture of Fear: Why Americans are Afraid of the Wrong Things* (New York: Basic Books, 1999).

16. Pinker, *The Blank Slate,* p. 317.

17. Glassner, *The Culture of Fear,* pp. 42–43.

18. Fowles, *The Case for Television Violence,* p. 76.

19. Reprinted in James Twitchell, *Preposterous Violence: Fables of Aggression in Modern Culture* (New York: Oxford University Press), p. 139.

20. Anonymous, "Col. Crockett Beat at a Shooting Match," in *The Tall Tales of Davy Crockett: The Second Series of Crockett Almanacs, 1839–1841,* ed. Michael A. Lofaro (Knoxville, Tenn.: University of Tennessee Press, 1840), p. 11.

21. Borgna Brunner, ed. *TIME Almanac 2003* (Boston: Information Please, 2003), p. 362.

22. Tamar Lewin, "Study Finds No Big Rise in School Crime," *New York Times,* 20 March 1998, Sec. A, p. 20.

23. I know this sounds incredible. Anyone who doubts it can check it out on the Internet or read Colin Wilson's account, "The Strange Crime of Issei Sagawa," in *Apocalypse Culture II,* ed. Adam Parfrey (Los Angeles: Feral House, 2000), pp. 6–27. Be warned, however—the latter reprints the actual photographs Sagawa took of his dismembered victim.

24. Emily Eakin, "An Unabashed Extremist of Sex and Violence," *New York Times,* 2 March 2003, Sec. 2, p. 19.

25. Norbert Elias and Eric Dunning. *The Quest for Excitement* (Oxford: Blackwell, 1970), p. 31 and Alfred Hitchcock, "Why 'Thrillers' Thrive," in *Hitchcock on Hitchcock: Selected Writings and Interviews,* ed. Sidney Gottlieb (Berkeley, Calif.: University of California Press, 1997), p. 111.

WORKS CITED

•

Abbott, Geoffrey. *The Book of Execution: An Encyclopedia of Methods of Judicial Execution*. London: Headline Publishing, 1994.

Allen, Hervey. *Israfel: The Life and Times of Edgar Allan Poe*. New York: Farrar & Rinehart. 1934.

Andrews, Raymond L. "Grandfather Liked Them Gory." *Esquire*. Feb. 1950. pp. 56–58.

Anglo, Michael. *Penny Dreadfuls and Other Victorian Horrors*. London: Jupiter, 1987.

Auguet, Roland. *Cruelty and Civilization: The Roman Games*. London: George Allen & Unwin, 1972.

Brownlow, Kevin. *Behind the Mask of Innocence*. Berkeley: University of California, 1990.

Burke, Edmund. *A Philosophical Enquiry into the Origin of Our Ideas of the Sublime and Beautiful*. Oxford: Oxford University Press, 1990.

Burt, Olive Woolley. *American Murder Ballads and Their Stories*. New York: Oxford University Press, 1958.

Callahan, John M. "The Ultimate in Theatre Violence," in *Violence in Drama*, 165–175.

Charney, Maurice. "The Persuasiveness of Violence in Elizabethan Plays," in *Renaissance Drama: New Series II,* ed. S. Schoenbaum. Evanston, Ill.: Northwestern University Press, 1969. 34–51.

Collison, Robert. *The Story of Street Literature: Forerunner of the Popular Press*. Santa Barbara, Calif.: Clio Press, 1973.

Cooper, David D. *The Lesson of the Scaffold: The Public Execution Controversy in Victorian England*. Athens, Ohio: Ohio University Press, 1974.

Cuming, E. D. "Blood Sport" in *The History of Popular Culture,* ed. Norman F. Cantor and Michael S. Werthman. New York: Macmillan, 1968. 295–300.

Dalziel, Margaret. *Popular Fiction 100 Years Ago: An Unexplored Tract of Literary History.* London: Cohen & West, 1957.

de Viragine, Jacobus. *The Golden Legend: Readings on the Saints,* trans. William Granger Ryan. Princeton: Princeton University Press, 1993.

Denning, Michael. *Mechanic Accents: Dime Novels and Working Class Culture in America.* New York: Verso, 1987.

DeVries, Leonard. *'Orrible Murder: Victorian Crime and Passion.* New York: Taplinger, 1971.

Diehl, Huston. "The Iconography of Violence in English Renaissance Tragedy," in *Renaissance Drama: New Series XI,* ed. Douglas Cole. Evanston, Ill.: Northwestern University Press, 1980. 27–44.

Douglas, Ann. *Terrible Honesty: Mongrel Manhattan in the 1920s.* New York: Farrar, Straus and Giroux, 1995.

Dundes, Alan. *The Study of Folklore.* Englewood Cliffs, N.J.: Prentice-Hall, 1965.

Elias, Norbert and Eric Dunning. *The Quest for Excitement.* Oxford: Blackwell, 1970.

Ellis, Edward. *Seth Jones, or, The Captives of the Frontier,* repr. in *Popular American Fiction: Dime Novels,* ed. Philip Durham. New York: The Odyssey Press, 1966.

Emeljanow, Victor. "Grand-Guignol and the Orchestration of Violence," in *Violence in Drama,* ed. James Redmond. Cambridge: Cambridge University Press, 1991. 151–163.

Fiedler, Leslie. *What Was Literature?: Class Culture and Mass Society.* New York: Simon and Schuster, 1982.

Foucalt, Michel. *Discipline and Punish: The Birth of the Prison,* trans. Alan Sheridan. New York: Vintage Books, 1977.

Fowles, Jib. *The Case for Television Violence.* Thousand Oaks, Calif.: Sage Publications, 1999.

French, Philip. "Violence in the Cinema." *The Twentieth Century,* Winter 1964–1965, pp. 115–130.

Freud, Sigmund. *Civilization and Its Discontents,* trans. Joan Riviere. London, 1930; rpt. New York: Dover, 1994.

Gatton, John Spalding. "'There Must be blood': Mutilation and Martyrdom on the Medieval Stage," in *Violence in Drama,* ed. James Redmond. Cambridge: Cambridge University Press, 1991. 79–92.

Gerould, Daniel. *Guillotine: Its Legend and Lore.* New York: Blast Books, 1992.

Gilbert, James. *Cycle of Outrage: America's Reaction to the Juvenile Delinquent in the 1950s.* New York: Oxford University Press, 1986.

Glassner, Barry. *The Culture of Fear: Why Americans Are Afraid of the Wrong Things.* New York: Basic Books, 1999.

Goldstein, Jeffrey H., ed. *Why We Watch: The Attractions of Violent Entertainment.* New York: Oxford University Press, 1998.

Gonzalez-Crussi, F. *Suspended Animation: Six Essays on the Preservation of Bodily Parts.* New York: Harcourt Brace, 1995.

Gordon, Mel. *The Grand Guignol: Theatre of Fear and Terror.* New York: Amok Press, 1988.

Gottlieb, Sidney, ed. *Hitchcock on Hitchcock: Selected Writings and Interviews.* Berkeley, Calif.: University of California Press, 1997.

Gurr, Ted Robert. "Historical Trends in Violent Crimes: A Critical Review of the Evidence," in *Crime and Justice: An Annual Review of Research,* ed. Michael Tonry and Norval Morris. 295–353. Chicago: University of Chicago Press, 1981.

Gutjahr, Paul C. ed. *Popular American Literature of the 19th Century.* New York: Oxford University Press, 2001.

Halttunen, Karen. *Murder Most Foul: The Killer and the American Gothic Imagination.* Cambridge, Mass.: Harvard University Press, 1998.

Haining, Peter. *The Art of Horror Stories.* London: Souvenir Press, 1976.

———. *Sweeney Todd: The Real Story of the Demon Barber of Fleet Street.* London: Robson Books, 1993.

———. *The Classic Era of American Pulp Magazines.* Chicago: Review Press, 2000.

Hindley, Charles. *Curiosities of Street Literature.* London: The Broadstreet King, 1966.

Hollingsworth, Keith. *The Newgate Novel 1830–1847: Bulwer, Ainsworth, Dickens & Thackery.* Detroit: Wayne State University Pess, 1963.

Houseman, John. "What Makes American Movies Tough?" *Vogue.* January 15, 1947, pp. 88, 120, 125.

Jacobs, Frank. *The Mad World of William M. Gaines.* Secaucus, N.J.: Lyle Stuart, 1972.

Jones, Gerard. *Killing Monsters: Why Children Need Fantasy, Super Heroes, and Make-Believe Violence.* New York: Basic Books, 2002.

Kellerman, Jonathan. *Savage Spawn: Reflections of Violent Children.* New York: Ballantine Books, 1999.

King, Stephen. *Danse Macabre.* New York: Everest House, 1981.

Laqueur, Thomas W. "Crowds, carnival and the state in English executions, 1604–1868," in *The First Modern Society: Essays in History in Honour of Lawrence Stone,* ed. A. E. Beier, David Cannadine and James M. Rosenheim. Cambridge: Cambridge University Press, 1989.

Lawrence, D. H. *Studies in Classic American Literature.* New York: 1924; rpt. New York: Viking, 1964.

Legman, G. *Love and Death: A Study in Censorship.* New York: Hacker Art Books, 1949.

Lofaro, Michael A., ed. *The Tall Tales of Davy Crockett: The Second Nashville Series of Crockett Almanacs 1839–1841.* Knoxville, Tenn.: University of Tennessee Press, 1987.

Mast, Gerald and Bruce Kawin. *A Short History of the Movies,* 8th Edition. New York: Longman, 2002.

McCall, Andrew. *The Medieval Underworld.* London: Hamish Hamilton, 1979.

Morley, Jackson, ed. *Crimes and Punishment: A Pictorial Encyclopedia of Aberrant Behavior.* Vol. 18. London: BCP Publishing, 1974.

Neuberg, Victor E. *Popular Literature: A History and Guide: From the Beginning of Printing to the Year 1897.* New York: Penguin, 1977.

Nye, Russel. *The Unembarrassed Muse.* New York: The Dial Press, 1970.

Panofsy, Erwin. "Style and Medium in Motion Pictures," reprinted in *Awake in the Dark,* David Denby, ed. 30–38. New York: Vintage Books, 1977.

Pearson, Edmund. *Dime Novels.* Boston: Little Brown, 1929.

Pierron, Agnès. "The House of Horrors." *Grand Street,* 57, No. 1, 1996. 87–100.

Pinker, Stephen. *The Blank Slate: The Modern Denial of Human Nature.* New York: Viking, 2002.

Praz, Mario. *The Flaming Heart: Essays on Crashaw, Machiavelli, and Other Studies in the Relations between Italian and English Literature from Chaucer to T.S. Eliot.* Gloucester, Mass: Peter Smith, 1966.

Reynolds, David. *Beneath the American Renaissance: The Subversive Imagination in the Age of Emerson and Melville.* New York: Knopf, 1988.

Ryan, John K. "Are the Comics Moral?" *Forum* 95, 1936. pp. 301–304.

Sante, Luc. *Low Life: Lures and Snares of Old New York.* New York: Vintage, 1991.

Seneca. *Seneca: Four Tragedies and Octavia,* trans. E.F. Watling. London: Penguin, 1996.

Skal, David J. *The Monster Show: A Cultural History of Horror.* New York: W. W. Norton, 1993.

Smith, Gene and Jane Barry Smith. *The Police Gazette.* New York: Simon & Schuster, 1972.

Spierenberg, Pieter. *The Spectacle of Suffering: Executions and the Evolution of Repression from a Preindustrial Metropolis to the European Experience.* Cambridge: Cambridge University Press, 1984.

Stade, George. Review of Wendy Lesser's *Pictures at an Execution. New York Times Book Review,* December 1, 1994, p. 10.

Starker, Steven. *Evil Influences: Crusades Against the Mass Media.* New Brunswick, N.J.: Transaction Publishers, 1989.

Steranko, James. *The Steranko History of Comics,* Volume One. Reading, Penn.: Supergraphics, 1970.

Tatar, Maria. *The Hard Facts of the Grimms' Fairy Tales.* Princeton: Princeton University Press, 1987.

Thompson, Harold W. *Body, Boots, and Britches: Folktales, Ballads and Speech from Country New York.* Syracuse, N.Y.: Syracuse University Press, 1979.

Tuchman, Barbara. *A Distant Mirror: The Calamitous 14th Century.* New York: Ballantine Books, 1978.

Turner, E. S. *Boys Will Be Boys: The Story of Sweeney Todd, Deadwood Dick, Sexton Blaks, Billy Bunter, Dick Barton, etc.* London: Michael Joseph, 1948.

Twitchell, James. *Preposterous Violence: Fables of Aggression in Modern Culture.* New York: Oxford University Press, 1989.

Wardtop, Daneen. *Emily Dickinson's Gothic: Goblin with a Gauge.* Iowa City: University of Iowa Press, 1996.

Zaks, Richard. *An Underground Education.* New York: Doubleday, 1997.

INDEX

•